pierced in the Heart

The Miracle of
Healing after
GRIEF and LOSS

Bonnie J. Brooks

PIERCED IN THE HEART
Copyright © 2014 by Bonnie J. Brooks

Author photo copyright © 2014 by Gabrielle Légère, GP Photography

All rights reserved. Neither this publication nor any part of this publication may be reproduced or transmitted in any form or by any means, electronic or mechanical, including photocopying, recording or any information storage and retrieval system, without permission in writing from the author.

Unless otherwise indicated, all scriptures taken from the Holy Bible, New International Version®, NIV®. Copyright © 1973, 1978, 1984, 2011 by Biblica, Inc.™ Used by permission of Zondervan. All rights reserved worldwide. www.zondervan.com The "NIV" and "New International Version" are trademarks registered in the United States Patent and Trademark Office by Biblica, Inc.™ Scripture quotations marked (NLT) are taken from the Holy Bible, New Living Translation, copyright © 1996, 2004, 2007 by Tyndale House Foundation. Used by permission of Tyndale House Publishers, Inc., Carol Stream, Illinois 60188. All rights reserved. Scripture quotations marked (CEV) are from the Contemporary English Version Copyright © 1991, 1992, 1995 by American Bible Society. Used by permission. Scripture quotations marked (NIrV) are taken from the Holy Bible, New International Reader's Version®, NIrV® Copyright © 1995, 1996, 1998 by Biblica, Inc.™ Used by permission of Zondervan. All rights reserved worldwide. www.zondervan.com The "NIrV" and "New International Reader's Version" are trademarks registered in the United States Patent and Trademark Office by Biblica, Inc.™ Scripture quotations marked (KJV) are taken from the Holy Bible, King James Version, which is in the public domain.

Some individuals' names have been changed to protect their privacy.

ISBN: 978-1-4866-0367-1

Word Alive Press
131 Cordite Road, Winnipeg, MB R3W 1S1
www.wordalivepress.ca

Library and Archives Canada Cataloguing in Publication

Brooks, Bonnie J., author
    Pierced in the heart : the miracle of healing after grief and loss / Bonnie J. Brooks.

Issued in print and electronic formats.
ISBN 978-1-4866-0367-1 (pbk.).--ISBN 978-1-4866-0368-8 (pdf).--
ISBN 978-1-4866-0369-5 (html).--ISBN 978-1-4866-0370-1 (epub)

    1. Brooks, Bonnie J. 2. Brooks, Bonnie J.--Health.
3. Spiritual healing--Christianity. 4. Christian biography--Canada.
5. Abused women--Canada--Biography. I. Title.

BT732.56.B76A3 2014	234'.131092	C2014-901396-5
		C2014-901397-3

"Tragedy, dysfunction, abuse, addiction, perseverance, victory, forgiveness, peace, and love. Bonnie Brooks takes us through these deep waters in her memoir, *Pierced in the Heart*. How does a five year old deal with the tragic loss of her mother? Bonnie, driven by a desire to help others, shares the painful journey of her life from tragedy to victory and love. A powerful read."

—Tom Blubaugh,
Author and Literary Strategist
Night of the Cossack
www.tomblubaugh.net

"*Pierced in the Heart* begins with unfathomable tragedy, but it emerges on the other side as a tale of blazing courage and a series of beautiful vignettes of the love of a Savior who longs for His children to be restored. As a woman who has suffered many years in silent shame hiding my bipolar disorder, I found Bonnie's book to be like applying a healing salve to years of misplaced feelings of guilt and regret. The raw, unfettered honesty with which she so bravely weaves her story maintains authenticity while directing our gaze heavenward to the Mighty Counsellor who binds our wounds and sets the captives free!"

—Kate Davis,
Blogger at www.dedikated2love.com

"Bonnie Brooks's memoir is deeply moving. She brings you into a world of deep mental pain, self-destruction, tragedy, and then triumph. Anyone who has ever lost someone to suicide will feel the power in her work. Brooks demonstrates how the ripple effect of one single act impacts an entire family for decades. At the moments when you feel the deepest despair, there is healing and hope. Bonnie's story is inspiring, showing that no matter what our life experiences are, we can transcend them and go on to help ourselves and others."

—Dr. Sheri Kaye Hoff, Ph.D.,
Best-selling author of *Keys to Living Joyfully* and
Be the Inspiration: 7 Ways to Inspire Your World
www.lifeisjoyful.org

"*Pierced in the Heart* is much more than a book—it is a lived-out life. Bonnie describes the unfolding revelation of her personal journey. She shares not only the wounds of her heart but also how she has been liberated and how her experience of God's "kiss" has impacted the course of her life. Bonnie's insights inspire me to live the life I only dream about and how it is possible, though broken and wounded, to dance a new dance by being still long enough to hear God whisper to my heart. So long as I practice this one thing, I will never be the same."

—Donna Kutzner,
Author of *Dancing on the Wings of the Wind* (forthcoming)

"Bonnie has told a very personal story of discovery, understanding, and healing. It takes courage to be open and honest with ourselves. It has been proven time and time again that this is the only way to heal: we cannot heal or change what we do not acknowledge. Bonnie's story proves this—she has learned to let go and move on. This book will bring many readers to the realization that suffering is cured when we acknowledge our past, deal with it, and let go. Bonnie's journey has not only changed and transformed her life, it has saved it. Reading this book may well be the catalyst that saves others!"

—Bob Outhwaite,
Choices Seminars Facilitator (1996-2002)

"I am in awe of Bonnie Brooks' tenacious strength. Bonnie's story and writing style took me on a guided tour into the darkest corners of life that people seldom talk about, making it possible for me to personally experience the horror of many kinds of loss. Even after twenty-three years as a pastor and ten years of work at Choices Seminars, where I have watched countless people come to terms with loss and healing, the book has still profoundly impacted my appreciation of the pain that many people suffer in silence. The best part for me was my front row seat where I could observe the powerful commitment it takes to rise above it all and carry on and, at the same time, cheer for the joy of Bonnie's healing. *Pierced in the Heart* is an encouragement to all who need to find hope and healing from the stories that often remain hidden deep in their memories."

—Bill Spangler,
Pastor, Life Coach,
Choices Marketing Staff (2002–2012)

Dedication

I dedicate this book to my God, who is always with me, when the sun shines or when it rains, when I am on the mountaintop or in the valley, when I feel his presence or when I feel alone.

I thank God for the messages he whispered into my heart and mind as I wrote this book. He spoke to me more clearly than ever before in my life. His healing words helped me come to terms with deep pain from my past and to let go of wounds that held me back for so long.

Contents

Foreword	xi
Introduction	xix
Part One: We Are All Wounded	1
1. Childhood Wounds	3
Part Two: Death	15
2. You Know How She Died, Don't You?	17
3. Please Help the Family Over This One	29
Part Three: Relationships	45
4. You Deserve Better Than This	47
5. Harsh Words Bring Tears	59
Part Four: Health	73
6. You Are Clinically Depressed	75
7. I'm Not Depressed, I'm Just Tired	97
8. Fall from the Top	113
Part Five: Learning to Let Go	129
9. Making Choices	131
10. Going with the Flow	139
11. Trusting God	149
12. Breaking down Heart Walls	155
Afterword	165
About the Author	169
Resource Links	171
Acknowledgements	173

Foreword

What if life is truly a journey and not a destination? That would mean there are many paths to be taken.

During my many years as a successful Texas businesswoman, I often wondered why employees and friends practiced so many self-defeating behaviors. I dreamed of helping people use the tools I had developed in business to learn to live with clarity and passion. In 1983, I invited Dr. Phil (McGraw) and his father, Dr. Joe McGraw, to join me in designing and presenting experience-based seminars that asked a simple question: "If better is possible, is good good enough?" The purpose was to show that people could live their lives at a hundred percent.

After conducting the seminars together for ten years, I left the partnership and formed Choices Seminars, expanding on the tools I had already developed. The purpose of each seminar was to bring healing and change the world one heart at a time. I have worked with thousands of people every year in North America who leave my program committed to a purpose-filled life, one of joy, passion, peace, and abundance.

Bonnie Brooks attended a Choices seminar in Calgary, Canada, several years ago. She recently told me she had written a book that contained information about the Choices program and asked if I would review it and give permission for her to include my name and some examples of what took place in the program. She also asked me to provide a short endorsement if I liked what I read.

As I read Bonnie's manuscript, I was thrilled to see how beautifully it interwove many of the concepts she had learned at Choices. She wrote about how my presentation on the wounds of the heart spoke to her so intensely, resulting in a major transformation in her life.

The underlying theme of Bonnie's story is how heart wounds held her back from experiencing a joy-filled life until she made the choice to let go of those wounds so she could live a life of purpose. Her personal story is very compelling. Her heartache, each circumstance followed by reconciliation through the words God spoke to her, make for an inspiring story.

I read Bonnie's manuscript on a trip to Mexico where I went to rejuvenate in preparation for another year of serving participants at the Choices program. Within the first hour of starting to read, the story gave me chills. I read her graphic portrayal of tragic events that happened in her life and I connected with how true those events are for so many people. It reminded me that we too often pass each other by and never share our pain or know how much someone else is hurting. I had not even finished the complete manuscript before I contacted Bonnie and told her I would like to write the foreword to her book rather than the short endorsement she had requested.

Based on the extensive work I do in the personal growth area, I have listened to thousands of individuals pour out buckets of tears and words of anger as they share their own devastating life experiences. However, for Bonnie to write such a gripping story, to be so open in an arena far greater than the Choices room, takes tremendous courage.

Several chapters are devoted to suicide and mental health challenges in Bonnie's immediate family, including her own experience with depression and bipolar disorder. The book illuminates for readers that mental illness is a widespread health issue in North America, yet it is typically shrouded in an eerie silence. Too often, people carry the heavy weight of their own illness (or that of family members) without support from the broader community. Until more people speak out about the challenges of mental illness, the stigma will continue. It is a choice to remain silent, fearful of judgment or ridicule. It is also a choice to speak out to impact change in a positive way so others living in silent pain come to realize they aren't alone and can do something to improve their own situation.

Bonnie agonized over whether or not to publish the graphic chapter on her past marriage, but I encouraged her not to delete it because the message is so important. I was pleased to learn that her former husband granted permission to include it in the book. That must have been an important breakthrough for him in facing his own past and taking a step forward to a more hopeful future. The chapter illustrates how abuse carries on from generation to generation. Most wives believe when they are abused that it is "my fault" or that "I deserved it." Perhaps this will help them see it differently.

Until more women are willing to share the story of abuse that continually perpetuates itself, the cycle will continue. At the same time, the book gives insight into what the abuser may have experienced that brought him to such a negative approach in dealing with his own past pain. But the book does not make excuses for the abuser any more than it makes excuses for the abused individual to continue to subject him or herself to abuse. Both parties have the option to make better choices for their lives.

The last section of each chapter, where Bonnie converses with God, is very powerful. Sometimes she asks matter-of-fact questions. Sometimes her heart cries out for answers to help her make sense of her life journey. In facing her Maker with an authentic desire to understand and gain lessons from her past, Bonnie experienced healing words from God—some gentle, some candid—but they all helped her see that life is, indeed, about choices. Those choices are at times personal. At other times, they are choices in a broader sense, where humanity as a whole has chosen actions that cause a ripple effect through the ages on the lives of others who come after them. As I read those interchanges, I was deeply touched by the overflowing love of God for his children and his tenderness in caring for each of us in our personal journey, even when we do not sense his presence in our lives.

Bonnie has a beautiful gift of words and I know her book will benefit you. If you are open to improving your own life, you will read words that resonate personally, bringing you in touch with your deepest self. You may come to appreciate that even seemingly minor events have caused heart wounds as deep as major events in your life. You will also realize in a profound way that if you choose to hold onto your past, it will affect your ability to live a life of wholeness. Regardless of the magnitude of heartaches you have experienced, you can choose to leave them behind, as this book so poignantly points out, and take a path that leads to the life of purpose that God wants for you.

I cannot heal or change what I do not acknowledge.

Be. Do. Have. *Be* committed to *do* what it takes to *have* what you want.

Thelma Box

—Thelma Box
Creator and Founder of Choices Seminars
Changing the World One Heart at a Time
www.choicesseminars.com

*Sometimes God redeems your story
by surrounding you with people who need to hear your past
so it doesn't become their future.*

—Jon Acuff [i]

---

i Jon Acuff, *Twitter*, "Sometimes God redeems…" June 22, 2011 (https://twitter.com/JonAcuff/status/83520550550507520).

Introduction

Give God your mess and let it become your message.
—Joyce Meyer[ii]

Wounds of the heart go deep. My mother lay in a pool of blood on an ambulance cot from a self-inflicted knife wound to the heart. In her intense pain, she cried to my father, "I'm sorry, Stuart, I didn't mean it." Tragically, that brutal self-assault resulted in her death. My mother's actions pierced the hearts of four young children and our dad, affecting all of us throughout our lives.

This is the story of several facets of a challenging life journey. It is also an awakening to how, through God's healing power, I am now able to forgive and figuratively embrace the woman who, even in death, influenced so many aspects of my journey.

---

ii Joyce Meyer, *Twitter*, "Give God your mess ..." November 16, 2013 (https://twitter.com/JoyceMeyer/status/401764144962994176).

Wounds of the Heart

A white-haired, solemn-looking woman stood at the front of the room. I sat in the middle seat in the first row surrounded by sixty other participants from all lifestyles—individuals who like me had come to this safe place to look in the mirror and gain the tools they needed to live a life of joy and fulfillment.

It was the second morning of that unique five-day personal development seminar. Thelma drew a stick person on chart paper and stated in a matter-of-fact way that wounds of the heart have scarred all of us. With each example, she made a mark with a felt pen on the stick person's heart. As I listened and watched, that felt pen appeared as a knife in her hand.

Each mark became profoundly personal for me—my mother's suicide, my brother's suicide, other family mental health issues, an abusive marriage resulting in divorce—with the knife piercing deeper and deeper. The longer Thelma spoke, the more my body heaved as I sobbed, trying to hold the pain inside and wishing I could hide in a corner where no one would see or hear me.

Thelma said that it starts when we are young, when someone says or does something that causes pain to our innocent and sensitive hearts. She spoke of how the wounds, fresh and raw at first, gradually start to heal and close up. But then they open again as new hurts emerge. Finally, scar tissue builds because of the number and intensity of wounds. When that happens, it becomes difficult to open our hearts to anything tender or beautiful again. Sometimes the wounds are so deep that we cannot stand the pain, so we put up thick walls—heart walls—and do not allow anything to break them down.

In the few minutes of that illustration, I realized that Thelma was talking about me, my life, my coping mechanisms, and my ways of protecting myself. I knew my heart wounds had turned into scar tissue. I knew that heart walls had blocked so much happiness and joy from my life. Was I willing to spend five days being vulnerable enough to let go of the wounds? Was I willing to gain the tools I needed to get more of what I was longing for in life?

I committed to "play hard" during that program. As a result, I learned to make choices that helped my wounds begin to heal. Over time, however, I discovered there were still many wounds to deal with, some that I did not know had existed, some new ones that surfaced, and some layers still peeling off from old wounds.

Turn your wounds into wisdom.

—Oprah Winfrey[iii]

Resurrecting a Dream

How did I get to the next level of healing in my life? Strangely enough, it resulted because I was broken, physically, due to a serious household accident. Shortly after returning to my job, complications from the injury required me to take almost one more year off work. During that time, I reflected often on the longings of my heart. I had pushed those longings deep down inside because of other choices that kept me constantly busy, but not completely

---

iii Oprah Winfrey, *ThinkExist*, "Wounds quotes," December 19, 2013 (http://thinkexist.com/quotes/with/keyword/wounds/).

fulfilled. I had always wanted to write a book, and that desire began to tug at me—a reminder of promises I had made to myself years earlier.

I began reading and participating in online programs about writing. Early one morning, I received an email about a book-writing retreat. It almost shouted at me to enroll. By that time, I had just re-entered the workforce on a part-time basis, so it didn't seem practical to take time off work again. But how could I resist? I signed up, and during the two months of anticipation before the retreat began, I tried to figure out what I would focus on in my upcoming book. I couldn't decide. Ideas continued to drift in and out of my head.

Around this time, I listened to an intriguing teleseminar in which the speaker shared her approach to writing. She said that she started each writing session by saying, "I wonder what my spirit says today about…" She then jotted down ideas on various aspects of her life that came to mind. I decided to try something similar as soon as I woke up each morning, writing down the words, "God, what is your spirit telling me today?" I waited until thoughts surfaced and translated into words on the page during short writing stints. What I wrote was mainly individual collections of thoughts, as God gave me insight on various topics. I didn't write anything that even hinted at the skeleton of an entire book.

During this time, I also began to pray about the upcoming retreat, telling God that I only wanted to write something that would bring honor to him. I told my pastor about my plans and asked him to pray the same prayer for me. But when the first day of the retreat arrived, I still didn't have a plan for what to write. Would my dream be resurrected or buried again?

I wrote the first draft of this book during that writing retreat. Like an earlier personal development seminar I attended, it was a healing experience. Tom, my writing coach, guided me through the process, but I also underwent several treatments with Lori, a myofascial release physiotherapist. She assisted me in dealing with the extreme physical pain I was experiencing during the retreat, some of it from my recent physical injuries, some from a lifetime of holding onto trauma.

The dream began to come to life as I participated in breathing exercises and visualizations to prepare me for writing. With my eyes closed and an unspoken question in my heart—"God, what is your spirit telling me today?"—I waited and listened for his voice. When it came, I wrote quickly, sometimes joyfully, sometimes tearfully.

At the end of five intense days, my labor pains were over and my manuscript was born. Like a baby, it still needed a mother's time and attention before it would grow to maturity. I was almost as excited as the day I held my newborn daughter, Tara, in my arms. It wasn't the book I had expected to emerge, just as my ruddy-faced, dark-haired daughter wasn't what I envisioned Tara would look like. Tom had said it was better if we didn't know in advance what we were going to write, that it was better for the message to come from our hearts. He said that the book would write itself and the pen would be just the instrument to paint the picture that was fully exposed on the inside, on the heart. The heart would breathe to life all that lay within, waiting for full exposure to the world.

A Healing Journey

I sometimes struggled in my writing journey, but now the picture that was previously hidden in my heart, seen only by God, has been revealed in this book.

Parts of it may be painful to read, just as they were painful to write. It begins as a story of loss—of family members, relationships, and my own health. But don't despair and quit reading if it makes you sad at the beginning. Look for the diamond in the rough that continues to be cut and polished, because the beauty in this story emerges as layers of scar tissue are gradually cut away. It ends as a story of triumph—of letting go, acceptance, and joy.

God gave me a priceless gift as I questioned him about traumatic and challenging life situations. Many of my questions were really cries to God about the grief of my unhealed wounds. In response, His whispered words of healing are sprinkled throughout each chapter, with a section at the end of each called "Healing Words and Letting Go." Those words flowed silently from his heart to mine in response to the questions I asked.

I cannot claim that the words I wrote are literal words from God, but I can say that I internalized the words on the page in my heart as messages from him. He opened my mind to new perspectives I had not considered before. He not only helped me to release my own heart wounds to him for healing, but also illuminated the wounds of other people who have influenced my life. This gave me a deeper understanding of their life struggles. I, in turn, have been able to forgive those who have hurt me deeply through their actions.

I will restore you to health and heal your wounds.
—Jeremiah 30:17

part one
We Are All Wounded

A pearl is a beautiful thing that is produced by an injured life… The treasure of our being in this world is also produced by an injured life. If we had not been wounded, if we had not been injured, then we will not produce the pearl.
—Stephan Hoeller[1]

---

1 Stephen Hoeller, *Beliefnet*, "Inspirational Quotes", December 19, 2013 (http://www.beliefnet.com/Quotes/Health/S/Stephen-Hoeller/A-Pearl-Is-A-Beautiful-Thing-That-Is-Produced-By-A.aspx).

chapter one
Childhood Wounds

I will never fail you. I will never abandon you.
—Hebrews 13:5 (NLT)

BLOODY BED SHEETS

I walked sleepily to my parents' bedroom late one night, a tiny blonde-haired five-year-old. I have no memory of what woke me up, no recollection of sounds that disturbed my sleep. But when I got there, no one was in the room. All I saw was blood splattered on the bed. I didn't know it then, but it was my mother's blood.

My next memory is of my dad sitting in the overstuffed armchair in the living room. I likely didn't know the meaning of the word "slumped," but over time that word has resonated with the picture of my dad. He was slumped in the armchair. I remember nothing else of that night, no memories of whether my sister and two brothers woke up, no sight of my mother, no sound of screaming sirens, and no commotion in the house. Just bloody bed sheets and my dad slumped in the armchair.

Abandoned

The next thing I remember was meeting a new family. My three siblings—Faye, Campbell, and Stuart Jr.—and I arrived at the home of Aunt Katharine and Uncle Rix and their three teenage children—Hugh, Gwen, and Don—on a dark winter night. They crowded around us in the small kitchen, trying to make us feel welcome.

The only image I hold in my mind is that of my aunt. Aunt Katharine was a large woman, and she was scary because she had big dirty arms. *Why wouldn't she wash them and be clean?* I wondered. Over time, I learned that Aunt Katharine's arms weren't dirty. Dark splotches called freckles covered them completely. That was nothing to be afraid of for a five-year-old, soon to be six.

We didn't know it, but after our mother died, Dad planned to have us stay with his sister for only a few weeks until he could arrange for a housekeeper to come in and care for us while he worked. There were four of us, ages seven, six, five, and two. Dad worked nights. Who would want to be responsible for us on a full-time basis? Apparently no one did, because the few weeks with our aunt and uncle stretched into four and a half years, until Dad remarried.

I have always known that my dad loved me deeply, but I never felt a sense of security and peace as a young child. I remember Dad being gone, working late hours, even before my mother died. I have cherished one fond memory of those days all my life. Dad called me his little Bonnikins and sang me a song called "Pretty as a Rainbow" (Harry Belafonte). I actually believed Dad had written it just for me.

Oh, to have a dad who was always there! He abandoned us, too, unknowingly, when our mother killed herself. He remained in our hometown after she died. When his plan to arrange for a housekeeper didn't work out, we gained a new family and a new life. Dad seldom came to see us, as he was busy with work at a time when a two-hundred-mile trip was almost a full day's journey. I know he tried, but he didn't try hard enough. Would it have been different if he had known the importance of a father's bonding relationship with his children?

One day during the writing retreat when I left for a physiotherapy appointment, Tom, the writing coach, sat on a sofa with his soon-to-be six-year-old daughter snuggled up against him. The moment he told me her age, I pictured another child lying there. Another soon-to-be six-year-old who never had what Skyla had—the security of knowing her dad was there for her. Skyla lay contentedly, feeling secure and protected, knowing that her dad would always be there, encouraging her to live the best life she could. How I ached to have a memory like that, which might have carried me through the hard times of life.

Working on the Puzzle

For years, I operated in snippets of time, searching my memory in an attempt to piece together all the puzzle pieces. When did I learn that my mother had died? Who told me she died of a heart attack? Why had blood covered the bed sheets if she had died of a heart attack?

Throughout those years, I dutifully filled out the forms at the beginning of each school year: Name of Father, Name of Mother, Siblings… One line even asked if any family members were deceased, a word that I had discovered meant "dead." I filled in the word "Mother." Then, on the line where it asked for the cause of death, I wrote "heart attack." Yes, every year I wrote a lie about how my mother had died. I hadn't known it was a lie—a lie my dad had told me.

My early years in school were relatively uneventful. I transferred from my Grade One class in one city to another city several hours away when I went to live with my aunt and uncle. I played with other children at recess in the playground and chattered with them in class whenever the teacher turned her back. I was outgoing and played with the neighborhood children, but I don't recall having anyone I could call a real friend.

One day, a classmate invited me to meet her near our school on Sunday so we could walk back to her house to play. I waited in anticipation of forming a new friendship. The long, dragging minutes turned into half an hour. She never showed up. The excitement of having someone who wanted to be my friend faded with every passing minute until I dejectedly turned around and walked slowly home. That was my first memory of feeling rejected. I felt unworthy of becoming someone's friend, or being a friend. Was it a wound of the heart? Was this one of the cuts of the knife in Thelma's illustration, a small wound that affected me deeply?

Had my mother rejected me? Absolutely! Had I known it in those early years? No, not outwardly. That rejection was buried so deep inside that I wasn't consciously aware of it. Do I know it now? Sadly, yes! And I understand the implications of that rejection, which have played themselves out throughout my life.

I have come to realize that my mother's death impacted many aspects of my life: my feelings of self-worth, my treatment of others and how I allowed them to treat me, my friendships, and my marriage and family relationships.

In looking back, I clearly see that the thread of her violent action was interwoven into the very fabric of my being. It was a very strong thread, resisting my efforts to remove it for most of my lifetime. I sometimes still find pieces that need to be removed, but I'm thankful that I am gaining the tools to pull them out more easily.

> *It does not work, it is dysfunctional, to deny that our childhood wounds have affected our lives.*
>
> —Robert Burney[2]

Joy and Sadness

My two brothers, sister, and I lived in a safe environment for four and a half years. It was a strict atmosphere with lots of rules and responsibilities, but those years with Aunt Katharine, Uncle Rix, and their family contain the best memories of my childhood. Every summer, we went to my uncle's sawmill and the four of us ran free, explored, and played happily.

Perhaps this time was a gift to help heal the losses of our earlier years when our mother left us abruptly in death, and our dad left us almost as abruptly when he gave our aunt and uncle temporary guardianship over us. Dad visited when he could and heaped presents on us. We knew deep inside that he loved us, and one summer he even loaded us into the car full of camping gear and took us on a vacation to the lake. That was a very special two weeks of my life.

---

[2] Robert Burney, *Joy2MeU*, "Inner Child Healing Techniques," December 19, 2013 (http://www.joy-2meu.com/InnerChild.htm).

Almost as suddenly as it began, that time with my aunt and uncle ended. Dad remarried and he and his new wife, Amy, uprooted us from the sanctuary that had become home. We stood outside by Dad's car that summer day in my aunt and uncle's driveway, feeling a mixture of excitement in going to live with Daddy again and sadness at leaving behind what had become our family.

I saw the tears in Aunt Katharine's eyes as we prepared to leave. I now understand the wounds of her heart, having four children torn away from her, children she had learned to love, children she had helped transform from unruly, undisciplined little neighborhood bullies and thieves into happy children, full of adventure.

My aunt told me a few months before she died that she regretted that she might have been too hard on us. She began playing the "if-only" tape, blaming herself for things that had happened to us over the years. I told her she could not have done anything more to give us a good life.

And how could I blame my dad? During all that time of separation, he must have ached to have us with him. Sometimes only in letting go can we make the right choices. He knew that having us stay with our aunt and uncle was probably best for us. After he remarried, he wanted us with him so he could make a happy home for us.

Unfortunately, a recent marriage, with a new baby on the way, is a difficult adjustment for anyone. Adding to that scenario four children not much younger than Dad's youthful wife resulted in a tough family situation for all of us. The initial excitement of having a home where we thought we would be accepted and loved soon vanished.

I picture Thelma with her felt pen marking another wound on the stick person's heart as she continues to illustrate the effect of different circumstances on our lives.

SIX PIERCING WORDS

In looking back on middle school and high school, I recall significant moments that etched themselves onto my inner being, screaming loudly that I was not worthy—of friendship, of even young teenage love. Those messages came in the form of unkindness and rejection from other students, and even hurtful or thoughtless actions of teachers.

By the time I reached high school, I was no longer the happy and talkative child of my earlier years. I was shy and introverted, and had only one close friend. My friend and I looked enviously at the popular students constantly surrounded by others clamoring to be part of their social sphere.

The most memorable incident that affected my self-worth took place in my Grade Eleven English class. My teacher was Miss Mooney, a tall, willowy, gray-haired, and stern woman. I was an excellent student in the humanities and did well in her class. One day, Miss Mooney taught a lesson on free verse and then gave us a corresponding writing assignment to complete. My pen flew along the page. I felt like I was free, just like the name of the poetry form we were exploring. It was wonderful to feel so liberated at a time in my life when I felt so constrained by my environment. I knew my writing was a masterpiece. I knew Miss Mooney would give me a high mark because I had written so expressively. As I excitedly handed in my paper that day, I could hardly wait for our next class.

Before returning the graded papers the following day, Miss Mooney stood to the left of my desk near the front of the room. She read one poem, my poem, pronouncing each word slowly and precisely. I was ecstatic. She was going to praise me, and the whole class would be awed by my creative work. In my mind danced images of the popular kids surrounding me after class, raving about what I had written, and opening a door for me into their inner circle.

Miss Mooney finished reading and paused with deafening silence. I waited for her congratulatory words. She finally spoke, but the words were all wrong: "This is an example of plagiarism."

Had I heard her right? Sadly, I had!

Those six words pierced my heart—six words to destroy my belief in myself. Then she gave the whole class a lecture on plagiarism. As I slid down into my seat with my head bent low, I wondered if the others knew she was speaking about my poem.

Confusing thoughts swirled in my mind: *But it's my original work. Maybe it isn't. Maybe I read it somewhere else and wrote the words from memory. I guess I can't write after all. How could I think I could really write a masterpiece like that? I'm not good enough. I must be a cheat.*

I did not have the confidence at the time to challenge her comments in class, or even privately. I was fighting to keep my head above water in a pool of fifteen hundred other high school students. I was struggling to keep from drowning in a sea of self-doubt and low self-esteem. I was clawing for a life preserver in that crowded pool but found nothing to grab onto.

I expect some students had life preservers—strong family connections, supportive friends, self-esteem nurtured throughout their lives in a family where they knew others loved them. But I hadn't experienced that. My stepmother, Amy, only twenty-eight years old, had three young children of her own by this time—Denise, Bruce, and Debbie. She had no energy or capacity to throw me the lifeline that would have helped me survive my tumultuous teen years. Dad didn't know how to express his feelings and connect with his children, so I didn't have the resources I needed.

As a result, I sat in Miss Mooney's English class and kept silent. I didn't fight for the mark I deserved. I accepted the failing grade and carried with me a wound of the heart that screamed, "Cheater." I continued to vacillate between wondering if what I had written was, in fact, my original work, and knowing deep inside that I was really an unacknowledged winner.

Miss Mooney left a deep wound that remained for many years. It's only scar tissue now, but it's a reminder that I believed I wasn't good enough, in spite of the fact that I had performed well in school overall.

What about all those students who struggled harder than I did? What did they do with the wounds they carried every day? How many of them succumbed as they fought to keep their heads above water, to keep breathing and surviving the institution of high school?

I have wondered at times what heart wounds caused some teachers to treat students in hurtful ways instead of protecting and nurturing their hearts. Instead they put these students down and devalued them, telling me that those teachers were hurting, too, fighting battles with low self-esteem, likely because of their own circumstances.

I hope over time they learned the importance of discovering and encouraging the hidden seeds of greatness in all their students, so the young people entrusted to them didn't experience the pain and humiliation I did the day I heard those six piercing words.

Healing Words and Letting Go

God, as I look back on my childhood and youth, I realize that my mother and father left me feeling insecure when they abandoned me. I see that it was hard for me to form friendships, and that some of my teachers didn't inspire me to believe in myself. Many of those hurtful events contributed to my dim view of adult role models and resulted in choices I made as I matured.

I realize, too, that all your children have wounds. Major physical or emotional damage, or seemingly insignificant events, can have a profound effect throughout our lifetimes. I can see now that most of the experiences that affected me deeply were minor, yet I allowed them to hold me back from living confidently and pursuing a life of purpose.

Why is there such a range of reactions to life situations by different people? Why do some children who lived with devastating circumstances emerge from childhood into strong and resilient adults? Why do they face the world with hope for their future and forge lives of significance? Why do others succumb to those same types of situations? Why do many with the advantage of families who loved them deeply, who didn't experience negative childhood conditions, make such poor choices in adulthood?

I have tried to make sense of these questions over the years as I observed how people deal with different life events. So much of it, I just do not understand.

My child, *go back to the very beginning, to the story of creation (Genesis 1–3). I had just finished fashioning a beautiful world called Earth and I declared that everything was good—all my handiwork, including the creation of man and woman. They had the best of everything. They hadn't dragged any heavy baggage along from a miserable childhood.*

Everything they needed and could have imagined surrounded them. I continually showered them with love. I gave them a healthy and stimulating living environment and a purpose in life. They couldn't make excuses about their lives being ruined because of mistreatment or health issues. They couldn't blame bullying and negative influences from their friends.

They could have kept it all and lived forever. Yet they lost everything—the intimate relationship we had, their perfect garden home, their health, and eventually life itself. Why? They made a choice that has affected all of humankind throughout history.

They chose to walk away from the beautiful relationship we had. First, they went to the tree I told them to stay away from and ate the fruit I told them not to touch. They questioned that I wanted only the best for them. They ran and hid from me when I tried to repair the broken connection between us.

Earth's story is now one of shattered relationships and heart wounds interspersed with repaired relationships and heart healing. You, my child, are a part of that larger story. You are the author of your life and can choose what your book says.

You can decide if you want our relationship to be magnificent or dull, deep or shallow. I am willing to guide your life and heal your heart wounds, if you'll let me. I am willing to be the thread of hope interwoven throughout your story, bringing new meaning to every difficult circumstance of your life.

The choice, my child, is yours.

God, as I read these words and reflect on them, all I can say is, yes, I choose to be open to you. I want to be the author of a story that speaks of healing, not of shattered relationships. I want to learn what it means to be whole. I know that will only come if I allow you to guide me and heal the wounds of my heart.

> *The past does not have to be your prison. You have a voice in your destiny. You have a say in your life. You have a choice in the path you take.*
>
> —*Max Lucado*[3]

---

[3] Max Lucado, *When God Whispers Your Name* (Dallas, TX: Word Publishing, 1994), 110.

part two

Death

Grief is a choice. You have to choose to let grief in. You have to allow it. You have to allow yourself to feel it... Grief is the key to your spiritual growth.

—Rick Warren [4]

---

[4] Rick Warren, "Getting Through What You're Going Through, Part 2," August 10–11, 2013. Sermon at Saddleback Church, Lake Forest, California.

chapter two

You Know How She Died, Don't You?

What you need to know about the past is that no matter what has happened, it has all worked together to bring you to this very moment. And this is the moment you can choose to make everything new. Right now.

—Charles Swindoll[5]

PARTY TIME

In university, my life consisted mostly of studying, working, and partying. I was a server in a restaurant, with tips making up most of the money that helped pay my way through school. I enjoyed being part of the work crowd, which was also a very social crowd.

In my first year of post-secondary studies, I skipped many classes and spent a lot of time learning to play bridge and hanging out in the education building's cafeteria. After that year, I moved into an apartment with my older sister, Faye. There I lived the party

---

5 Charles Swindoll, *World of Quotes*, "Charles R. Swindoll Quotes," December 19, 2013 (http://www.worldofquotes.com/author/Charles+R.+Swindoll/1/index.html).

lifestyle, left behind guys twice my size in chug-a-lug beer-drinking contests, and experimented with drugs.

I somehow convinced both my friends and myself that I was the center of the social scene. It didn't take many months before our landlord gave Faye and me an eviction notice, and we spent a cold New Year's Eve carrying our belongings down the street to another apartment building with the help of some friends. Fortunately for us, the new landlord hadn't checked our references.

I lost focus in school, even though I had wanted to be a teacher ever since the age of five. I took a year off school to work more, party more, travel more, and try to find myself. I spent much of that time working in a restaurant and being treated like a second-class citizen even though I was as intelligent as most of the clientele. That experience sent me back to university. I felt a renewed sense of purpose, to becoming the teacher I had always dreamed I could be.

LSD

During the four-month summer break after my second year of university, I worked and partied again. Early that summer, I met Spence when I was hitchhiking one evening. He introduced me to a drug I had not experienced before. Its street name was LSD.

LSD! The first time I heard the word was when Faye came home from a psychology class and told me about an experimental drug that gave people hallucinations and caused other strange effects. As soon as she told me about it, I knew that my insatiable curiosity would drive me to try it someday. With Spence as my guide to the world of hallucinogens, someday was here.

My first LSD trip… how do I describe it? Do I describe it? I don't *want* to describe it, other than to say that my face contorted in unimaginable ways as I gazed in the mirror, my eyes existing only as black holes. Strange sounds and sights immersed me—inside me, in front of me, around me. Music enlightened me as it spoke in ways music had never spoken to me before. One song in particular, "Time Is," created a beautiful day, just like the name of the band (It's a Beautiful Day).

But the beautiful day became an ugly day as I attempted to escape from the world I was living in, if only in my mind. Some of the sounds, smells, and images became grotesque. I tried to find my way back to a place of safety and peace. I lived through twelve hours of this experience and wondered if I would survive.

When I did, I went back for more. Why? Was I curious? Looking for acceptance? Looking for a way to escape my own life, which I didn't know was so full of intense pain? Sometimes after I came down from a high, I would sit and listen to music—the same music over and over—wondering what I was doing with my life, wondering when and where I might find a place of goodness and healing. How could I escape the emptiness and thawing of my insides that gave me such unimaginable agony?

Faye and my closest friend and roommate, Gerrie, were worried about me. They knew I was in a dangerous place. They wanted to rescue me from myself but didn't know what to do. I avoided them as much as I could, because I didn't want them to know what I was doing and what I was feeling. I was afraid of what was happening to me as the deep black pit pulled at me. I kept going back to stand near its edge, allowing myself to be drawn closer and closer to its depths.

The last time I used drugs was the night when Spence and his friends brought out something even better than LSD. A few people in the group began to shoot up heroin. I was already high on LSD, but I knew I had to try heroin, too. I also knew that if I did, it might destroy me. Even in my drug-induced state, I knew what it could mean. I wanted to take it anyway.

I stood in the living room at the home of Spence and his roommate, fighting for my turn. Even though they were high, somehow they knew it would be dangerous for me to mix heroin with what I had already taken, so they refused to let me have any. I tried to take the needle out of someone's hand, but others held me back.

And so I suffered the loss of a way to ease the deep pain I didn't fully comprehend. Was I simply trying to alleviate pain in the short term? Or was I trying to end it permanently? I don't have an answer for those questions, but I do know that I'm alive today, and that's all that really matters.

The next morning, I was still stoned. The party was finally over and Spence dropped me off at my apartment. The LSD from the night before, laced with amphetamines (speed), kept me from coming down from the high. My heart was racing so fast that I didn't know how to slow it down. I feared I might have a heart attack. I decided to go for a ride on my motorcycle. It was a beautiful day. Would the beautiful day, the sunshine, and the morning smells calm my soul? I hoped they would.

The Final Puzzle Piece

For some reason, I finally ended up at my cousin Gwen's house. I stopped and got off my motorcycle, then walked up to the door, my

Chapter Two: You Know How She Died, Don't You? • 21

heart still racing. I knew the large black holes remained where my eyes belonged. I wondered if Gwen would notice, but I needed to talk to someone, and she was home.

Gwen was one of the three older cousins we had lived with after my mother's death. I don't know what we talked about initially, but something in our conversation provoked her to say these life-changing words: "You know how she died, don't you? She killed herself."

Gwen was talking about my mother. No, I hadn't known how she had died. According to all the forms I had filled in during my school years, she had died of a heart attack. That was all I knew from the time I was old enough to question her death. With Gwen's words exploding in my mind, I clearly pictured a puzzle called "My Life." One piece had been hazy and out of focus all these years—the piece depicting my mother's death.

I figuratively picked up that puzzle piece, Gwen's words still hanging in the air. As I looked at it, the image became crystal clear. I placed it where it belonged. The puzzle was complete. No need to wrestle anymore with things that didn't make sense, such as why there had been bloody sheets on my parents' bed if my mother had died of a heart attack. I had rationalized it from the time I learned of the cycles women go through each month. That must have been the reason for the blood.

Now I learned that she had stabbed herself with a knife. She had hidden behind a door, in a disturbed mental state, initially planning to stab my dad.

Pierced in the Heart

It was both bewildering and heartbreaking for me to come to terms with what my mother had done to herself and her family. I tried to talk to my dad about it, but he wouldn't engage in conversation. I talked to my sister, Faye, and she told me she had never believed our mother was dead. Faye thought she had gone away as she had so many other times, and that she would come home again someday.

Unfortunately, at that time in my life I had no understanding of mental illness. I hadn't even considered that my mother might have had mental health issues. My way of trying to make sense of how she could have taken her life so horrifically was to write a poem:

Pierced in the Heart

You stood,
The steel-sharp knife
Clutched in your hand.
A cruel game you played.
You didn't mean to cut
So deep, I think,
Perhaps your way
Of having someone notice you.
But then the knife slipped in.
It pierced your heart
And you lay dead

Upon the floor.[6]
Now many years have passed
And he who you hurt most,
Who suffered torment,
Grief and self-rebuke,
Has eased his pain,
And filled his hours again
With laughter, love, and life.
But you—non-entity—cease to exist!
Not true—
You still exist within my thoughts,
Continue in your haunting ways.
You pierce my heart a thousand times.
Sometimes I question why
And ponder at your fate,
But know there's nothing I can do.
It's twenty years too late!

"I'm Sorry, Stuart; I Didn't Mean It"

I wonder now what effect my mother's death had on me, both her actual death and the immediate aftermath of it. What did I see, hear, touch, smell, and feel the night she died? What wounds did I receive the night when that knife pierced her heart and ended her life? What residue remains?

---

[6] I learned years after writing this poem that my mother did not die immediately after stabbing herself. She was taken alive by ambulance to the hospital before she died.

What wounds of her heart caused that knife to go in? She said to my dad in the ambulance on the way to the hospital, "I'm sorry, Stuart; I didn't mean it." Didn't mean what? The fact that she was hiding behind the door when Dad came home from work that night, holding one of his new chef's knives in her hand, waiting to stab him with it? The fact that he, her husband, had to escape for his life? The fact that she turned the knife on herself, knowing as she lay on the ambulance cot that she was going to die, leaving him to care for her four young children who would no longer have a mother in their lives?

What was she really thinking? That she didn't mean to leave her husband alone so many times while she was dealing with her own struggles? That she didn't mean for him to have to answer phone calls at work from their children and to listen to them say, "Daddy, Mommy's gone again" and then for him to rush home to four young children abandoned again?

Did she say it because she had told her children stories that sent fear into their hearts, fear that the house was going to blow up because she had spilled turpentine down the air vent? Or that the strangler was going to come into our home, the strangler that the newscaster spoke about who lived three thousand miles away?

Was she sorry because she had never wanted children and that she tried to give me up for adoption before I was even born? Was she sorry that she abused and neglected us and that she didn't hug and comfort us as a mother should? Was she sorry that she had let her young children run wild, stealing and beating up other little neighborhood children?

What did my mother mean? There are a million words in those seven words—a million words written across my heart that have cut as deeply into my core as the knife that pierced her heart.

> *In most cases, suicide is a solitary event and yet it has often far-reaching repercussions for many others. It is rather like throwing a stone into a pond; the ripples spread and spread.*
> —Alison Wertheimer[7]

MY MOTHER'S WOUNDS

She didn't survive, but I did. Why? We all have wounds of the heart. Were her wounds any more acute than mine? Why was there such a difference in how we coped with the challenges of life? What made her break?

Was my mother wounded, just like me? Was she wounded before she was born or as a young child? Her father had died during World War I and so she had no father figure in her life. Did that affect her self-esteem and coping skills?

My mother was the first child born to Grandpa and Nana, my grandmother. Did my grandmother have mental health issues like my mother? Did she abuse, neglect, and put fear into my mother as my mother had done to me? Does abuse always perpetuate more abuse?

---

[7] Alison Wertheimer, *A Special Scar: The Experience of People Bereaved by Suicide*, Second Edition (East Sussex, UK: Brunner-Routledge, 2001), 3–4.

I fought hard to give my daughter all the things I lost in my childhood. I wish someone had fought for my mother when she was a child. She must have carried her own wounds, just as I did. But why would she go so far as to kill herself? Questions… I have so many questions.

> *It is tempting when looking at the life of anyone who has committed suicide to read into the decision to die a vastly complex web of reasons; and, of course, such complexity is warranted. No one illness or event causes suicide; and certainly no one knows all, or perhaps even most, of the motivations behind the killing of the self.*
>
> —Kay Redfield Jamison [8]

HEALING WORDS AND LETTING GO

When I first heard the song "Always Be a Child" (Ray Boltz), I finally caught a glimpse of what it meant to know that I have always been loved unconditionally. The song tells of how God was with us the moment we took our first breath and when we first cried. It tells of how God continues to be there through every moment of our lives, loving us as his children no matter what choices we make in life.

When I grasped the meaning of the words of Jeremiah 1:5—*"Before I formed you in the womb I knew you"*—I came to realize that before I drew my first breath, God accepted me and loved

---

[8] Kay Redfield Jamison, *Night Falls Fast: Understanding Suicide* (New York, NY: Alfred A. Knopf, 1999), 85.

Chapter Two: You Know How She Died, Don't You? • 27

me, even at the same time as my mother wanted to give me up for adoption. That was incredibly healing for me.

God, I have tried to internalize those words in my adult life after many years of heartache and feelings of unworthiness. Sometimes, in spite of such assurance, I still struggle with believing that You love me through everything that has happened in my life. I want to live with Your joy completely filling me every day. I want to release the pain of past hurts, of wounds of the heart.

My child, for me to accept you means that I will always be there. I have always been there. My heart broke for you when your mother left you alone as a young child. You did not deserve that treatment. She should not have abandoned you. She should not have been suffering with mental illness that resulted in her taking her own life.

Just as I have always been with you, I was with your mother before she was born. I was with her during her happy times. I was with her during all those years of sadness, when she longed to be a different person.

And I was with her in the last minutes of her life as she fought her final battle. When she spoke those words to your dad, "I'm sorry, Stuart; I didn't mean it," she was in essence whispering silently in her heart to me, "I'm sorry, Father; I didn't mean it."

I was with her in the darkness. She felt the warmth of my hand in hers, and she felt the intensity of my love as I embraced her. She is in my care. She went through so much pain in her life that she couldn't cope with it anymore.

It has never been part of my design for my children to do things like that. I could have intervened when she picked up the knife, but I didn't. I know it is hard for my children to make sense of the tough situations people go through. I never wanted you to have those heart wounds.

You and your mother have both come from difficult circumstances. I have given you a place in my heart where you can heal from all the past, from all the hurts you have bottled up inside for all these years. You will always be a child in my eyes. Never, ever forget that.

The intensity of emotion I felt after God embedded the above thoughts in my mind was almost beyond comprehension. I had always held contempt for my mother's actions. I hadn't believed she warranted any kind of love or respect from me because of what she had done. But the God of the universe was telling me now that the woman who birthed me, who had impacted my life so negatively but so powerfully, was worthy of his warm embrace.

How could I do less? I figuratively opened myself to the woman who had lost so much—a life of happiness, cherished family moments, healthy relationships, children growing up, and grandchildren being born. She was God's child as much as I am today. How could I judge her the way I did? I have shed so many tears in coming to this understanding.

Thank you, God, for loving her and holding her close when she shut her eyes for the last time that dark winter night.

> *… when we forgive, we set a prisoner free and then discover that the prisoner we set free was us.*
>
> —Lewis B. Smedes[9]

---

9 Lewis B. Smedes, *Forgive and Forget: Healing the Hurts We Don't Deserve* (New York, NY: HarperCollins, 1996), x.

chapter three
Please Help the Family Over This One

People can never predict when hard times might come. Like fish in a net or birds in a snare, people are often caught by sudden tragedy.

—Ecclesiastes 9:12 (NLT)

WHERE NO ONE STANDS ALONE

The night before my younger brother died, he and I sat together talking and listening to the song, "Where No One Stands Alone" (Mosie Lister). The words speak of someone who feels desperately alone and cries out in the darkness for God not to turn away and hide his face. The songwriter asks God to take his hand and hold onto him so he will not have to be alone.

The next morning, Stuart Jr., only twenty-six years old, moved his car out of the driveway so I could get out of the garage and go to church. I backed up, pulled alongside him, and waved as he sat in his vehicle on the street. I drove off, and as I glanced in my rear-view mirror, I saw him pull back into the driveway and then into the attached garage. I thought he was going to warm up his car because of the cold weather.

When I returned from church, I saw exhaust fumes creeping out into the cold air from under the garage door. Strangely, although I had no idea of what he might do when I left home, I knew instantly what I was going to find. Stuart Jr.'s body was slumped against the steering wheel, with the motor still running.

The first thing I did was cry out, "God help me." Those words carried me through the next several days and kept me from collapsing under the weight of this devastating heartbreak.

After I had driven away that morning, Stuart Jr. went into the house to change into his favorite suit and get some paper to write his final farewell before going back to his car. Why did he end his life in my garage when he knew I would be the one to find him? The words he left for me in his goodbye note said, "Please help the family over this one." Why did he give me those words as my final remembrance of him?

I did help the family over that one—and the next one, and the next one. I was always the strong one helping other family members in crisis. Then I experienced my own depressive episode seven years later. I drove my own car into the same garage many times, looking through the rear-view mirror as the overhead door closed behind me. I fixated on the blackened circular mark where Stuart Jr.'s car had run for over three hours, the exhaust mark a tragic reminder of that cold winter day. I would toy with my car key, trying to decide whether or not to leave the car turned on as he had done.

Living through the Nightmare

On the day I found Stuart Jr. leaning over the steering wheel of his car, I knew he was dead. I stood with the garage door open—in the forty-degree below zero cold—staring as my neighbor loaded something into his car, thinking I didn't want to ask him for help because I hated the thought of disturbing him.

I called Dad at work, but he wasn't there, so I mechanically told his assistant, "My brother is dead." I then hung up and called 911. The dispatcher told me that emergency vehicles were on the way, but I knew an emergency responder wouldn't bring my brother back to life. I carried my sleeping two-year-old daughter Tara from my car into the house.

Emergency responders arrived—fire trucks, police cars, an ambulance... the street was full of them.

I saw one of my neighbors standing outside looking at the emergency vehicles and then looking toward the house. I recall standing in front of the bay window and looking back, facial expression blank, giving no acknowledgement that I saw him, no emotion.

Amid those memories are recollections of police officers talking to me, asking if I had found a note from my brother. I hadn't even thought to look for one, so they went to the garage to search the car. They found an unfinished goodbye note on the floor in front of the driver's seat. Stuart Jr.'s final words were just a scrawl across the page:

> *I regret I could not be the person I was capable of becoming. Please forgive me for my mistakes, if you will. I have no resentments or hard feelings against anyone and hold no grudges against anyone.*

The police officers asked me many other questions that I don't remember. I was in a strange space, operating on automatic pilot. I don't know how long they talked to me or if they were still there when family and friends arrived.

Finally, I was able to reach my friend Gerrie by phone. I didn't want to bother her, because I knew she had invited a guest over for lunch that day, but she came right away to help take care of my daughter and lend a hand in whatever ways she could.

It seemed like such a long time before anyone else got there. I don't recall everyone who came. My husband Gord[10] came home from wherever he had been. Then my dad arrived from his house in the country. I called my pastor and he came, awkward and not sure what to say or do. Finally, I reached my sister Faye, especially concerned at how she would react, because she and Stuart Jr. had been so close since childhood.

I felt little emotion as I dealt with what I had to over the next week, with people coming and going, phoning, bringing over food and flowers. My cousin Gwen stood with me in the bathroom the next day as I shed my only tears of the week. I told her how the horrible exhaust fumes from the garage still permeated the whole house. Gwen told me that there were no fumes—it was only in my mind.

My one recollection of joy during the initial period of shock was when Faye, along with Stuart Jr.'s estranged wife Jessie, and I worked on his obituary. We laughed at so many of the good memories we had—healing memories.

I wanted so badly to write in my journal or to express through poetry what had happened, hoping it would help me come to terms with this terrible tragedy. When I had faced difficult situations

---

10 My former husband has given permission to use his name. His second name, Gord, is included throughout to avoid confusion, since his first name is also Stuart.

before, I wrote. But all that eked out of my pen were the following simple words.

Stuart

Our pain is deep. We loved him so,
The loss we feel no one can know.
God, you must ache for what he's done,
You loved him too. He was your son.

After the funeral service and gathering at my home six days later, it was a huge relief when almost everyone finally left. Gord was getting ready to drive my uncle to the airport. Just before they left, I went to my bedroom and collapsed with exhaustion and sorrow.

Gord walked into the room and saw me crying. Instead of a hug or word of comfort, he said angrily, "What, are you going to do the same thing as your brother now?" His heartless, cruel words, heaped on top of the heavy weight I had carried for the past week, almost buried me. Heaving with pent-up emotions, I finally released the floodgates.

This was all part of the pattern I had lived with from the time Gord and I got married. It didn't seem abnormal at the time for him to treat me this way, but in looking back, I see how destructive his behavior was. How sad for him. How sad for me that he had no comprehension of, or compassion for, the devastation of what I had just lived through. Only when his own ninety-three-year-old mother died did I see tears in his eyes, as he came to appreciate the meaning of loss.

My Brother's Wounds

Are you listening, God? Are you hearing me, God? Do you really care, God? Did you care the night my younger brother and I sat listening to the song, "Where No One Stands Alone"? I know now that Stuart Jr. must have been struggling with deep despair on his last night on Earth. Was he crying out for you to take away the blackness that surrounded him just as the singer had done?

He had just lost his wife to another man, lost his job to a slow real estate market, and would be losing his home before long to a huge spike in interest rates. He was trying to find a way to go back to school so he could move on to chiropractic college. He had applied for, and was waiting for acceptance into, an upgrading program.

He had come back to Alberta after trying to reconcile with his wife in British Columbia, and he had no place to go. He stayed briefly with our sister Faye in the condominium she was renting from him, knowing a for-sale sign would soon tell the story that he couldn't afford to renew the mortgage.

During the last week of his life, Stuart Jr. stayed at my home. I remember how lethargic and unmotivated he seemed, lying on the couch for hours at a time. It was an extremely cold January, in the minus forties all week. I was a stay-at-home mom back then—cooking, cleaning, baking, doing volunteer work, and most importantly, spending time with my two-year-old daughter. Tara and I spent every morning and evening creating Bible stories from felt characters. We sang worship songs during those special times of the day. I invited Stuart Jr. to join us, but he declined.

I hoped that maybe, just maybe, the songs and stories he heard from the other room would resonate for him and would give him the desire to renew his relationship with God. He had recently said that he wanted to start going to church again. In fact, I asked if he would like to come to church with Tara and me on the morning of his death, but he said no. He had other plans. Other plans!

Stuart Jr. had such an unstable childhood. He was only two when he was left motherless. When we lived with my aunt and uncle, we older siblings did what we could to nurture him. We thought he was stronger than we were, that he was the most resilient, because he had us to support him. We didn't know then what research has discovered now about the effects of maternal deprivation on an infant's future emotional state. After bonding with our aunt for almost five years, Stuart Jr. lost her, too, when Dad uprooted us to live with him and his new wife.

He was a seven-year-old with a father who worked long, late hours and seldom took time to encourage him and demonstrate his love. He was a young boy with a stepmother whose arms were always full with another newborn, infant, or toddler; she never had time to focus on him. Stuart Jr. had to take care of himself and be mature beyond his years. He had no solid roots, no stability. As I reflect back, I picture Thelma with her felt pen, speaking rapidly of the extent of his wounds as she illustrates them with mark after mark on chart paper.

I Didn't Want the Numbness

When Stuart Jr. turned seventeen and finished Grade Eleven, he left the home where Dad and Amy's young family of five children— Denise, Bruce, Debbie, Dora, and Linda—lived. Stuart Jr. moved in with Faye and me, the same summer that I had crossed over into the world of hallucinogens. Soon after he arrived, Faye and Gerrie dragged me away from the influence of Spence, my drug-taking, drug-dealing friend. We took a vacation to British Columbia and spent some time at a hippie haven on Vancouver Island.

During the five days we stayed there, living in driftwood shelters on the beach, I spent most of my time staring at the ocean and pondering my life. What was I doing? I thought about the reality that I might have wanted to end my own life with heroin. If that had happened, no one would have ever known that I was trying to stop the pain—the emptiness, the craving for something I didn't have and couldn't describe. People would have only said it was an overdose, and that young people shouldn't take drugs.

I sat and watched the waters on the shore advancing and receding, and reflected on how I longed for a different life. I didn't know what I wanted. I just knew I didn't want the hurt, the isolation, the feelings—or lack of feelings—that I couldn't even put into words. Maybe it was the numbness. I didn't want the numbness.

I came to no resolution while I sat watching the ebb and flow of the tide. I sat with a sense of desperation, and sometimes fear crept in to remind me of my vulnerable state. I wondered what would happen to me on my return home. I couldn't go back to the life I had been living that summer, to the drinking and drugs. I was still dealing with the shock of finding out only a few weeks earlier about how my mother had died. Blackness encased me at times. I had a void in my life that I could not fill. I knew my life needed to change, but I didn't know what to do.

Reflecting back now, I wonder if I was experiencing a depressive episode without even knowing it.

Rediscovering God

Shortly after I returned home, Stuart Jr. and a cousin took a trip to the West Coast. I didn't know it then, but they had planned to be drug dealers. Both were only seventeen. Where did they get an idea to do something like that in a time before the drug-dealing lifestyle permeated our society so extensively?

They didn't stay away for long. When they came back, Stuart Jr. told me what had happened on their trip. He divulged that when he had been stoned on drugs one night, he met the devil. "Old Charley" offered a deal to him and said that he would give Stuart Jr. everything he wanted in life if he would become a drug dealer and do other things he directed him to do. It sounded similar to the story of young people being lured into a life of prostitution or ending up under the control of a major crime ring, with enticing promises to captivate them.

Whenever I think of my brother sharing that experience, I picture Jesus and Satan sitting on a rooftop after Jesus' forty days of fasting and prayer in the wilderness. Satan, waving his hand, said, *"All this I will give you… if you will bow down and worship me"* (Matthew 4:9). Jesus firmly replied, *"Away from me, Satan! For it is written: 'Worship the Lord your God, and serve him only'"* (Matthew 4:10).

Satan was trying to make a deal with my brother, just as he tried to make a deal with Jesus. But Stuart Jr., like Jesus, turned his back and said, "It is written…" He came home and told me that he was going to start going to church again, that he had realized what had transpired while he was in that hallucinogenic state. I decided that I, too, needed to revisit my roots: I had learned during my childhood that there was a God, even though I had abandoned him during my teen years. I thought that might be the answer to my recent turmoil.

Stuart Jr. and I began to go to church together, and both of us came to know a God whom we hadn't known as children. This time, my God was an amazing God, not a stern being whose sole purpose was to point us to rules that would make our lives miserable. This time, I learned the meaning of the song "My God and I" (Kalnin, Mohr, Apsit), which speaks of the joy of having a relationship with him.

Together, we sang and celebrated our love for God with a youth group at picnics, at the lake, at wiener roasts and campfires, and on camping trips to the mountains. My brother was younger than I was, but he was also mature because he had experienced deeply the light of God's goodness.

What happened to him? Why did he walk away after such an intense encounter, one that had opened his eyes to the reality of the powers of spiritual light and darkness in this world? Or *did* he walk away? People are so quick to judge what they see on the outside without knowing what is transpiring in someone's heart.

STUART JR. AND JESSIE

Stuart Jr. met and fell in love with a young woman named Jessie. She was everything to him. Was she a replacement for the lost mother, aunt-mother, and stepmother? A substitute for all the rejections of his past life, or was she a truly a soul mate to him? Did Jessie bring healing to that heart I didn't even know was wounded?

A few years later, Stuart Jr. and Jessie got married, two weeks before my daughter Tara was born. For the next two years, they spent a lot of time with Tara, her dad, and me. They loved Tara so openly, freely, and playfully; it was a joy to my heart. Then Stuart Jr.'s world turned upside-down as he struggled to build a real estate business in a declining market, with Jessie yearning to have a child and Stuart Jr. saying they needed to establish themselves first.

Something happened between them that summer. Jessie left Stuart Jr. and returned to the West Coast, where she had lived most of her life. He tried to reconcile with her by phone but didn't succeed. He moved out to be near her and attempted to reconcile in person, but she was already in a relationship with a former boyfriend. He wrote to me several times and told me what was happening. He asked me to keep praying for him because he was going through such a difficult time.

CASTLES IN THE SAND

What a terrible loss it was when Stuart Jr. died; it created a hole in my heart that has never been replaced. I would have no more opportunities to have him join us in family celebrations and special occasions or casual visits and chats on the phone. I long so often to have my little brother near me. He wouldn't be just a little brother now; he would be a brother I could turn to when I want to laugh or cry. I know that he would be strong.

Strong? Yes, we thought he was, but he still broke.

Sand Castles

Building castles in the sand,
A cliché heard a hundred times,
But that is what he did...
He built sand castles.
He longed for castles that were strong,
But sand can only stand
Where no winds blow or waters flow.
He built on sand.

THE BLAME GAME

How did I not know? As we sat talking that last night, how was I unaware that Stuart Jr. was thinking about what to wear when he turned the car key in the garage the next day? Earlier that evening, he had gotten up suddenly and said he had to go over to his own place to get some things, and that he would be back later. Is that when he decided exactly what he was going to do and when?

It was late when he returned, but I was still up waiting for him. We continued our conversation. We reminisced. He talked of the loss of his marriage. I shared some of the pain of my own marriage. We tried to make sense of it all, but we couldn't.

In retrospect, I realize he wasn't very talkative. He seemed preoccupied, deep in thought, and we listened to the music. The last song he heard in his life contained words about someone going through deep pain and a feeling of isolation, trying to break through the darkness to find God.

Chapter Three: Please Help the Family Over This One • 41

I have come to discover that there is never a wall holding us back from God. God is there in the darkness all the time, just as he was there when his own Son Jesus cried out to him, *"My God, my God, why have you forsaken me?"* (Mathew 27:46) Jesus experienced the isolation and fear, the feeling of lost hope, the enveloping darkness. I wonder if my brother had similar feelings. I know in my periods of darkness that it's all about lost hope, about not believing things will ever get better.

I didn't give my brother the hope and light he needed that night. I offered what I could, but it wasn't enough. I didn't know what he was thinking. I didn't know how fragile he was. I didn't know he was going to end his life the next morning.

> *Each way to suicide is its own: intensely private, unknowable, and terrible. Suicide will have seemed to its perpetrator the last and best of bad possibilities, and any attempt by the living to chart this final terrain of life can be only a sketch, maddeningly incomplete.*
>
> —Kay Redfield Jamison [11]

HEALING WORDS AND LETTING GO

God, that was such a hard time for me. I have blamed myself so many times for not being sensitive enough, wondering if I could have said something that would have made a difference, words that

---

[11] Kay Redfield Jamison, *Night Falls Fast: Understanding Suicide* (New York, NY: Alfred A. Knopf, 1999), 73.

would have resulted in my brother hanging on for another day, another week, another month.

My child, you don't have to be the strong one all the time. Let me carry the weight you have carried for so long. You are not responsible for the actions your brother took while he was going through all that pain.

God, I know you stood beside me when I found my brother in the garage slumped behind the wheel, when the carbon monoxide filled the space and the exhaust fumes permeated everything. I want so badly to let it all go, so healing can come.

My child, I, your Father, ached so much for you. I could see you trying to take charge of the situation, as you always do. You wouldn't even let your neighbor help, but he was a firefighter—he would have known how to help. I placed him there at that time so you would have someone nearby to support you, to hold you up and give you strength. But no, you always think you can do everything on your own. I hope that at this stage of your life you realize you can't.

Then you called your dad at work to let him know what had happened. When he didn't answer, you spoke to his assistant and he called your dad at home before you were able to. I want you to know that I was with your dad. You heard that he went into his bedroom and cried. Do you know that the last time he cried like that was when your mother died? It was good for him. I know he was hurting and that he needed to let it out to heal the wounds of his heart. He has gone through a lot of pain in his life and he never wanted to let others in. You must have picked up your strong, silent approach from your dad.

My Son cried when my children rebelled against me (John 11:35), and he cried on the cross when he felt abandoned by me. Don't you think that if your Lord Jesus cried, then it is all right for you, too? To be made in my image means having the beautiful qualities and traits that I have. It also includes the range of emotions I planted in people. For most of your life, you believed that it was wrong to be sad, wrong to be angry, wrong to cry, wrong to be joyful. You can rationalize all you want, but the fact is that I did create you and place all those feelings inside you.

Let's debate; I know you like to do that. What about anger, you say? Isn't that a sin? Yes, anger acted out in inappropriate ways is wrong. My children often use the emotion of anger in ways that hurt others. Look at you. You get angry now at times even though you didn't used to. You kept it all bottled up inside in your neat little compartment called Emotions I Can't Express, right alongside your other emotions of fear, sadness, and loneliness.

My child, I feel sad for you, and at the same time, I smile. How could you think it is wrong to feel? Feeling is what life is all about. Stop thinking, for a change. Experience life. Be free—cry, laugh, sing, and dance with joy. Love others and let all the delicious feelings I have created permeate your soul.

You like gourmet jellybeans. I've seen you buy bags of them and savor each flavor, some more than others. Some are hot—like the cinnamon ones that burn your tongue. Why don't you pretend that the gift of feelings I've given you is a bag of jellybeans? Don't just gobble them down. Take each one out and look at it. What color is it? What does it smell like? What does it taste like?

You may not like all of them—either jellybeans or feelings. Some aren't pleasant to experience, but experience them anyway. I've said to you, "Rejoice in the Lord always" (Philippians 4:4). Start rejoicing. Praise me for every experience that comes your way and every feeling that surfaces. Stop stuffing them back down inside.

Your life is more than half over, and you keep saying that you want to live fully. You cannot do it in some safe little cocoon or in an armadillo's armor. You need to come outside into the light and experience people, experience vulnerability, experience tears. You always want to be there for other people. You want to take care of them, but you never want to let them take care of you. Don't you think it's time to do that now? Try it. You will be amazed at how it makes you feel and how it changes you.

Seventeen years after Stuart Jr. died, I sat on the floor of my home office with all the sympathy cards and letters I had received after his death spread around me. As I picked up each card and read the words inside, I relived the intense grief. Afterward, I thought that my grieving must finally be over.

However, retelling the story now makes me feel even more overwhelmed than I did then. As I type with my eyes closed, the tears well up. As I absorb God's message for me, silent tears stream down my cheeks for a very long time and I cannot stop them.

God, today I can say that I experienced feelings just as you encouraged me to. I cried with an ache in my heart for the brother I lost, but I also cried with joy for the comfort you brought by encouraging me to feel all the emotions you created. In releasing my pain, I feel like I'm beginning to see daylight after the darkness.

> *Weeping may remain for a night, but rejoicing comes in the morning.*
>
> —Psalms 30:5

part three

Relationships

I suppose that since most of our hurts come through relationships so will our healing, and I know that grace rarely makes sense for those looking in from the outside.
—Wm. Paul Young[12]

---

12 Wm. Paul Young, *The Shack* (Newbury Park, CA: Windblown Media, 2007), 13.

chapter four
You Deserve Better Than This

*The secret of letting go is knowing that life will give you
something better than whatever it asks you to give up.*
—Guy Finley [13]

MARMITE IN THE WATER TANK

I never fantasized about a wedding, marriage, or family, as so many young girls do. As a young adult, though, I did go through the experience of questioning whether God wanted me to be alone for the rest of my life. Either that was not his answer or I misunderstood him, because at age twenty-four, I fell in love with Gord.

Unfortunately, the day of our wedding was the beginning of the end of our marriage. I had no idea that a man could contain so much rage. I had known him for five and a half years. After the wedding reception, we went to pick up the van he had camperized for our honeymoon and his mouth spewed vile words I had never

---

13 Guy Finley. *Life of Learning Foundation*: www.guyfinley.org. Excerpt from "The Secret of Letting Go" (http://www.guyfinley.org/free-content/video/4220). Used with permission.

heard before. Why? Simply because his brother and my sister had made a mess of the van.

I know that some of the mess was a bit extreme, like putting dark brown, gooey marmite into the water tank. But all the rest, including the honey smeared throughout the small refrigerator and across the walls, we could live with. I fought back tears at his parents' house as he continued to erupt like a volcano. His mother tried to calm me down, telling me that it wasn't a big deal.

Not a big deal? How could a man be so angry because of something so inconsequential? I asked myself that question for the next twelve and a half years as I lived with never-ending wounds of the heart. Years where knives repeatedly cut through, where pain never seemed to heal before another knife went in, deep and sharp.

By the third day of our honeymoon, I had started writing in my journal about the hopelessness I felt. Looking at the gold ring on my left hand, I wondered how I could spend the rest of my life with a man who was like a volcano, who said the cruelest things, the most outrageous and incomprehensible things.

During our marriage, I journalled and wrote poetry frequently, trying to make sense of something that made no sense and to find some degree of healing through writing. No words could express adequately the depths of my despair, the rawness, the ache inside that seldom left me during those long and torturous years.

Toxic Relationships

One week, my pastor preached about toxic relationships. As he spoke about how wrong it is to stay in a toxic relationship, I replayed

Chapter Four: You Deserve Better Than This • 49

some of the memories from my marriage. The pastor said that we need to walk away from those relationships.

I suffered mostly verbal abuse—filthy words, never-ending sarcasm and putdowns, uncontrollable anger—but sometimes it went beyond that to breaking things and physical abuse. One day, Gord shoved me to the floor in the upstairs hall. The next day, I went to the doctor because I was spotting blood.

"You're pregnant and you're going to have a miscarriage," said the doctor, emotionless. "Go home, go to bed, and wait until the fetus passes. Then go to the hospital."

From Friday until Sunday night, I stayed in bed while Gord made ongoing disparaging remarks. Finally, early Sunday evening, he told me that if I didn't get it over with soon, he would refuse to drive me to the hospital; he had to work in the morning and needed his rest.

At about 2:00 a.m., it was time. I had been sleeping in the guest bedroom. I dressed, went quietly downstairs, and opened the door to go to my car. Gord woke up and came down. He demanded to know where I was going. I told him that I was going to the hospital. He said, somewhat repentantly, that he would take me. He woke up and helped our three-year-old daughter get dressed, and we drove there in silence.

Throughout my life, unspoken grief has enveloped me during all the significant milestones of a second child's life that I missed. As I lay in the hospital bed that night, though, I was actually glad no more children would be coming into our home to endure the wrath of this man.

One morning, when there was no orange juice in the refrigerator, Gord went on a verbal tirade, a common reaction to anything that didn't align with his idea of what it meant for me to run a perfect household at all times.

His expletives matched his typical abusive rages and I finally said something I had never said before: "I don't need to put up with this anymore." I walked away quickly, up the stairs to our bedroom. He followed me in rapid pursuit, his words still flying through the air. I locked the door, then went into the bathroom and locked it, too. It didn't take much time for him to pick the locks of both doors.

His intense anger hadn't subsided and his fist came up—a huge fist that in the moment seemed larger than my head. His whole body vibrated with the fist poised to go through my face. I knew I was going to die that day and silently called out to God.

But something happened. His fist seemed frozen in the air, blocked by something invisible. I believe a stronger hand than his interceded and held him back. Finally, with obscene words still pouring out of his mouth, he turned and left—and I knew I was safe for another day.

I reported him to the police right after that incident. I asked what "assault and battery" meant. The woman I spoke with told me that what he had done was considered assault; if he had physically hurt me, it would have been battery. She told me how abuse escalates and how I needed to take care of myself. She suggested kindly that I either lay charges against him or get out of the relationship.

FISHING AND PUPPIES

Walk away? How do you walk away when you've been reeled in and tossed on the floor of a boat, flopping around with no way to get out?

My thoughts turned back to a canoe ride we took on a nearby lake before we got married. We were paddling through the reeds in a serene and beautiful place when Gord made a very strange comment that didn't make sense to me. "I think marriage is like fishing. Before you get married, all you want is the other person. But when you get married, it's like catching a fish. Once you've caught it, you don't want it anymore."

I couldn't grasp what he was saying. I shared my perspective on marriage, that it was just the beginning of a relationship, not the end, and that people grow to know their partners more and more over time. We were speaking foreign languages to each other, though we didn't know it at the time because we grew up in foreign cultures.

Even though I lived with three different mother figures and two father figures in three phases of my childhood and youth, I never observed any significant disrespect in the relationships between the adults in my life. The first day I experienced that was the day Gord and I married.

I learned only bits and pieces about Gord's childhood before our marriage. He was the oldest son in a family of three boys and two girls. His job was to be the protector—of his mother and his siblings. When the drunken father of those five children began his abusive tirades, Gord dragged himself out of bed at night to step in between his father and mother and take the blows directed at her. He was the one who interceded when his dad chased his mother around the house with a butcher knife. He was the one who kept his father out of his sisters' rooms at night.

That was what he knew. Men disrespected women. Rage—whether alcohol-induced or internally induced, for any reason—

was condoned. Men could turn their wrath on women to relieve themselves just as a puppy relieves itself on the floor or rug when it needs to go. No training required. At least puppies are trained and grow up and go where it is socially acceptable. They know their boundaries.

Why do these men, reeking of alcohol and with rage permeating every fiber of their beings, not learn better ways to relieve themselves? But that was Gord's unspoken excuse. He just perpetuated what happened in his own childhood. It was no excuse. He was not a puppy. He knew better. He could have chosen to take responsibility for his adult life and let go of his past.

Looking for Answers

I shared with my pastor how I appreciated him speaking about this subject, about toxic relationships. I told him that if I had heard a sermon like that long ago I might have escaped many years of anguish that began the night of my honeymoon.

During all those years, I was looking for answers, looking for someone to point me to solutions. All I got in my religious circles were the words, "Pray about it, and it will get better." I prayed until I could pray no more and the tears ceased to fall. I prayed about it until the pain in my chest—the vice grip on my heart—subsided. I put up thick walls to block out any feelings, just to survive each day. My heart eventually turned stone-cold—a chunk of ice—relieving the pain as the knives continued to pierce me.

I read all the books that existed on my bookshelves, my friends' bookshelves, and store bookshelves about abusive relationships. I continually looked for answers, but I never found them. I listened to Christian friends, pastors, and counselors tell me to stay with my husband, to keep living a Christian life because someday he would turn around and give his heart to God. I was told that if I didn't stay in my marriage, I was standing in the way of his salvation.

Choices! Gord made choices. Was I supposed to keep living with them? His choices were destroying me. I realize as I write this that the walls are still blocking my heart. Sometimes there is a small break, just a tiny hole in a dyke letting living water—goodness, love, and peace—flow through. But mostly, it seems I am still in a prison.

Marriage—A Prison Sentence

I was the prisoner of a cruel jailor. I couldn't say anything without being punished. I couldn't do anything without Gord's fury, which made me feel like I was always wrong, a worthless human being. He was always right. He had to do what he did to me because I made him do it. If only I hadn't done this, he wouldn't have to do that—get mad at me, yell at me, and abuse me verbally with words I had never heard before.

If only I had behaved differently, he wouldn't have had to squeeze my neck until I thought I was going to die. He wouldn't have had to shake his fist in my face until I thought it would explode into my head. He wouldn't have had to put his fist through the door, make a dent in the piano, or destroy my prized possessions. He wouldn't have had to make me shake uncontrollably inside, wondering when I was going to be like the door shattered right through the middle, unable to be repaired.

My jailor kept me in prison for over twelve long years. Some days, he was more reasonable and didn't walk in with rage oozing out as he turned the key in the lock down the hall. Some days he even seemed human; he seemed rational. Sometimes he even joked and laughed as if nothing were wrong.

Mostly, though, the moment he walked through the door, I could feel the negative energy saturate the room. I felt tentacles reaching toward me long before he physically came near. Those tentacles wrapped themselves around me and squeezed so tight that I thought the life would be taken from me. Then he came into the room and I greeted him, cautious, tentative, wondering when the next explosion would come.

Five Words

What held me back? Why didn't I just walk away? I had choices, too, and I made them. For over twelve and a half years, I made them.

The abuse finally caught up to me one night when I was talking on the phone with my stepmother. Gord was ranting in the background because I was on the phone. It was after nine o'clock at night. It shouldn't have bothered him, but it did. This was typical behavior for him anytime I talked on the phone. It was all about control. I started to repeat to Amy the words coming from his mouth. She was stunned. She and Dad had no idea what my husband was like. Around them, he always acted like the perfect son-in-law.

He did the same with his family and other people we knew. He verbally abused me at home and in the car when we went out, but the moment we walked into my parents' home, his parents' home, or the home of other family and friends, he changed before my eyes. His ugly tone turned loving and the words "dear" and "sweetheart" flowed from his lips. The rage inside him abruptly ended and he became Mr. Personality: friendly, laughing, and joking with those around him. To my close friends, I described him as Dr. Jekyll and Mr. Hyde.

Gord finally left the room and Amy said to me, "You deserve better than this." Those five words had more impact than all the words I heard from others and read in books about how to deal with an unhealthy relationship. Whether it was just my time or something else, I don't know. I knew I needed to preserve my safety and sanity.

Just over one month later, when I made it clear that I would no longer live that way, Gord finally agreed to pack his bags and leave. But I still breathed in the aftermath of his mistreatment for many years.

Walk Away

It seems that all my life I've made excuses for those who hurt me. Is it time to stop making excuses for them? Or is it time to free them with the understanding that they're only repeating the cycle of wounding others because of their own pain?

During a physiotherapy treatment, I told Lori that I had come to realize that people who treat others badly do so because they haven't healed from wounds to their own hearts. She replied that sometimes that's just where people are at in their lives. Yes, we all make choices. We choose to love, or we choose to hate, and those choices change inside us, sometimes within seconds of each other. What brings about the extremes of emotions people feel and the way they deal with others? How can someone be filled with rage one moment, abusing another person, then change into a tender, compassionate human being? What is it in the inner self that causes those extremes? Is it simply a battle of emotions? From a spiritual perspective, we explain it as the battle of good and evil.

If Gord were to come to terms with the unspoken ugliness of his own past and let go of his childhood wounds, I believe he would have happier relationships with others.

I'm not a counselor, psychologist, or psychiatrist, nor do I claim to have a deep understanding of the psyche or human spirituality, but I do know that I'm thankful that I finally walked away.

Healing Words and Letting Go

God, I thought I had finally healed from the pain of my marriage relationship when Gord, ten years after our divorce, said to me for the first time that he was sorry for the pain he had caused. But sometimes the deep hurts from those hard years resurface.

I want to let go of those wounds and walk away whole, with a forgiving heart. Help me to see this man through your eyes, God.

My child, you know part of Gord's story. You've heard of his childhood and think you understand what he went through. But you don't. You haven't even touched the surface of his experiences. To protect him, I will not speak all the details of shame he experienced from an abusive father.

Those abusive words that you heard in your marriage were the same words Gord's father subjected him to from the time he was an infant. At first, his father directed the words at his mother and Gord absorbed them subconsciously.

The imprinting was there. Every word, every inflection, every facial expression, every moment of terror he saw his mother go through was magnified tenfold, a hundredfold in that child's mind and became part of who he grew into.

It continued through his childhood and youth as he heard from his own father's lips what a despicable human being he was. He has borne those scars his whole lifetime. So much of the ugliness of what he said to you and others was simply a redirection of words he believed about himself.

As for the physical abuse, imagine Gord as a preschooler watching his mother being beaten and crying helplessly for it to stop. Picture him going to school and other children teasing him because of a swollen eye or large bruises across his face. Visualize him as a teenager black and blue from his father's vicious attacks as he tried to protect his mother, his siblings, and himself from those alcohol-induced rages.

Put yourself in the shoes of that young boy and feel the agony of betrayal he experienced when his own father sadistically killed his pet rabbits. His father was supposed to love, protect, and nurture him as a child, but all Gord saw, heard, and felt was a man who hurt and destroyed.

Gord's model, the father who should have guided him into becoming a respectful and loving husband to his wife and a nurturing father to his own child, was incapable of doing that. Instead, his father's childrearing and alcohol addiction caused that terrible cycle of disrespect and abuse to develop.

Yes, Gord and his father had choices, as does everyone on Earth. Why some people make choices to better their lives and others make choices to destroy others is beyond your comprehension. I know their hearts and I see into the deepest recesses of their beings. I see every wound of their hearts that made them put up walls and cause pain and suffering to themselves and their families.

You, my child, need to look at Gord through eyes of love instead of resentment and anger. Feel for his pain and the choices that brought misery to his life instead of joy. He was oblivious to how deeply he hurt others, so holding onto those experiences only hurts you now. Forgive him and let go of the wounds you received from him.

When God gave me this picture of Gord as a helpless child, it affected me deeply. I believed for years that his actions had resulted from the trauma he experienced as a child, but explaining his behavior using logic and reasoning was different than feeling deeply for that child and his pain. He was abandoned, too. In a different way than I was, but abandoned nonetheless.

How many years has it taken me to reconcile my hurts? It is an ongoing journey. How can I lay blame on Gord after comprehending more deeply what has gone on in his heart? I forgive him now for the residue of pain that remains.

God, I hand him to you to heal his heart wounds. I hope that—like a bulb planted in the fall lying dormant, then coming to life in the spring—the seed of goodness is growing inside him, ready to emerge through the ground when the darkness of his winter is over.

> *You will know that forgiveness has begun when you recall those who hurt you and feel the power to wish them well.*
> —Lewis B. Smedes[14]

---

14 Lewis B. Smedes, *Forgive and Forget: Healing the Hurts We Don't Deserve* (New York, NY: HarperCollins, 1996), 29.

chapter five
Harsh Words Bring Tears

The most important thing about a father is that he loves his daughter. The most important thing about a mother is that she loves her daughter.

—Tara Brooks, age seven

My Daughter's Wounds

Life was a struggle, both emotionally and financially, after my husband and I separated. Most of all, it was hard because of the hurt it caused my nine-year-old daughter. Tara's dad had subjected her to his tirades and constant sarcasm and putdowns of me on a constant basis. I had always vowed that if he ever started to treat her like he treated me, I would leave. It had been a balancing act between choosing to be a stay-at-home mom or leaving the relationship and being unable to remain at home to nurture Tara in the way I wanted.

I had weighed it off and on and felt that the positive influence I could have on her by being at home would counterbalance her dad's negative influence. But I was wrong. I have read that it takes eleven positive comments to counteract one negative comment. The negatives always outweighed the positives from Gord.

At first, Gord loved Tara and treated her as a doting father does. Then, because of something she did, or simply because he needed to vent, he began to injure his precious daughter, too. She was a beautiful child, innocent and pure, gentle but with an inner strength and resilience. Unfortunately, even that wasn't enough to protect her from the wounds to her heart.

Tara

Blonde-haired,
Blue-eyed child
Of tender years.
So quick to squeal
And clap with great delight.
Harsh words bring tears.

Yes, what Gord did affected Tara. Nothing could protect her from the hurts he heaped upon her. Even though he had not previously beaten down her tender spirit, she started to wear the scars as I did. I had to get out of the relationship and get her out with me before the damage became even more devastating.

Amy's five words, "You deserve better than this," spurred me to act both for my own well-being and that of my daughter. I had read that when abuse begins, it only escalates. Because I could see the pattern of Gord's abuse toward me—moving from swearing and sarcasm to deep emotional abuse to the beginnings of physical abuse—I knew that the same pattern would emerge with Tara. He had started by losing his temper and swearing at her, then hurting her with sarcastic words. Time would proceed to etch the deep wounds—emotional and physical—into her inner being.

Volcano Bubbling Inside

Tara has lived with it for a lifetime. You cannot escape the abuse if you have any contact with the abuser—and she did. She spent time with her dad on weekends and after school. Throughout her childhood and teenage years, I wondered how she could remain on such an even keel. She never got angry. She never got upset. She seemed happy. But I knew the volcano bubbling inside her would have to explode someday.

When it did, the timing was very bad for me. I was going through a difficult time because my dad had been very ill, up and down, in and out of hospitals. He was also suffering with dementia and just a few months from death. During that time, Dad was living with my sister, Debbie. He told her that he wanted to talk to a minister because he didn't know if God would forgive him for killing my mother.

Killing my mother? What did that mean? Had he really killed her? Had I been living with another lie for all these years?

I struggled to make sense of what was real and what wasn't. How could my dad have murdered my mother and gotten away with it? Wouldn't the police have discovered it through their investigation and put him in prison? Had he been in prison during the four and a half years we had lived with our aunt and uncle? Had he been given day passes to visit us? Could it really be possible?

Debbie was trying to understand it, too. After the pastor talked to Dad, he told Debbie that Dad said he felt guilty because he hadn't been supportive of my mother; he had left her alone to manage with four young children. He believed that his neglect had killed her, and he was deeply sorry for that.

It didn't end there for me, because his words resurfaced memories. Soon I was back in a state of angst over my mother's death. I have never used the word "mom," only the more formal "mother." That's what she was to me—a mother, never a mom. Oh, to be able to call her "Mom," but that word is too painful to say.

Mother, Did I Ever Laugh?

I was seeing a therapist, so I shared my confusion with him. He suggested that I go home and write a letter to my mother to bring closure to what she had done to me. I couldn't really grasp the concept of writing a letter to someone who was dead and who meant nothing to me. I told him that. I was glad she had died; if she hadn't, we four children would have become juvenile delinquents. That was my typical response when people told me they were sorry about what had happened to her. I said that she had never cared about any of us except Faye. The therapist told me to write the letter anyway, so I reluctantly agreed.

In the first part of my letter, I made excuses for what my mother had done, but the longer I wrote, the angrier I became. I began to realize the loss I had experienced in both her life and death. The next week, when I read the letter aloud to my counselor, tears poured down my face and my whole body shook.

Chapter Five: Harsh Words Bring Tears • 63

To my mother:

How can I even call you Mother? That word is so foreign to me. This letter may be all jumbled up, perhaps incoherent in places, but it's something I have to do. I have to communicate with you, for whatever reason. It's unclear to me right now what the reason is. Maybe, hopefully, I'll discover it as I write.

I've been going to counseling sessions for a month now and my therapist has given me an assignment—to write to you and tell you how I feel. How I feel? What does that even mean? "Do I feel?" may be the better question to ask. Because most of the time, I don't. Whatever you did to me as a child has been pushed so far down inside me that I wonder if there's really anything there.

What did you do to me? All I have are tiny pieces of my life that resurface from time to time. I keep trying to reach back to those five years of my life, to grab at whatever I can to make sense of who I am today.

I keep making excuses for you. You were ill. That's why you did what you did. You were probably desperately lonely and frustrated when Dad worked late so much of the time. Having little emotional support from him must have been tough. I know he wasn't much of a communicator, so that was probably really hard.

I know in my own marriage that I was so desperate to communicate with my husband, but he just kept shutting me out. I understand what that might have been like for you.

I've heard that you were a very creative person. You probably needed space and time and never had it because of us kids. I understand that, too. I wonder so many times if we're alike. Somehow I think we are, and that's kind of scary.

I think it's time to stop making excuses. It's time that I get to be the child. I never got that chance when I was young, and that's not fair. Why weren't you a mother to me? I was told that I should be angry with you for what you did to me, but I'm not. Maybe I will be later. Right now, I'm sad and hurt, or am I only sad? Usually when I'm hurt, I deal with it by getting angry.

Here I am, trying to write to you and express my feelings, and I can't even do that. Is it your fault? I think in some ways, it must be. You didn't love me. That's part of your job; it's something you should have wanted to do, or just done naturally.

Don't tell me you weren't capable of it, because I know you loved Faye. Even at five years old, I knew it, and Campbell knew it at six. We were jealous of her because we knew you loved her and didn't love us. You really messed up, because all that did was hurt Faye when you died. For almost twenty years, she didn't believe you were even dead. That wrecked her life and the relationship I should have had with her as a sister.

Why would you do something like that? You weren't a child. You were supposed to be an adult. You were in your mid-thirties before any of us were born. What did you have kids for anyway if your life was such a mess that you weren't capable of being a mother?

Why did you and Dad get married? Why did you leave him and take off. If things were so bad between you, why did you get back together and have us? Why did you ruin things so Dad had to quit chiropractic school just when he was ready to graduate?

Why did you treat Campbell so badly when he was a baby? Aunt Katharine told me that you would kick at him in his crib and that you would threaten to stick his head in the toilet when he cried. That is so sick!

I pity you. How many things have you done to me that I don't remember? You wanted to give me up for adoption to Aunt Katharine and Uncle Rix even before I was born. If that wasn't the ultimate way of telling me that I was nothing to you, what could be worse? Besides the fact that you rejected me sight unseen, you continued to reject me from the moment I was born. I wonder if there was even a moment when you actually cared.

Did you ever smile at me? Did you even once think that you loved me? Did you ever say those words? I don't think you did. When you rocked me as a baby, did you ever make me feel safe and secure? Or did you ever rock me? Maybe you just left me lying in the crib, crying to have my needs met, and did nothing. When Tara, your granddaughter, was born, I used to hold her close and she snuggled in, and I felt so good to be holding her and nurturing her.

I wonder how many times I lay there in wet or dirty diapers. I wonder if I lay there hungry or thirsty. I bet I did. And all that time, the messages that were being absorbed into the deepest parts of my being were that no one cared, that I was all alone.

What were you doing when I lay there crying? Were you playing with Faye? Were you kicking at Campbell? Were you lying in your room hating your life and your children? How many times did you say or think, I hate them. I wish they had never been born?

Did you ever play with me? Did you ever take me for a walk? What did you do for almost six years of my life besides give me messages telling me that I was nothing? I think about the joy of watching my daughter crawl and walk and run and talk and explore. I think about the happy times we shared in the first five to six years of her life. I loved to hear her laugh. It's the most beautiful sound in the world—a small child's laughter! Did I ever laugh? Did you ever make my life joyful enough for me to have a reason to laugh? And did you even care if I did laugh? I don't think you did.

I don't have any good memories of you. Don't you feel any kind of shame or guilt for what you did? What kind of legacy is that for your children—a mother of four children who gave us nothing but negativity? That's pretty pathetic. That's pretty disgusting. I'm glad I'm not like you.

What were you thinking when you took off and left us kids home all alone? I remember Stuart Jr. sitting in his highchair. The picture is as clear as day. Faye spoke into the phone, "Daddy, Mommy's gone again." What kind of human being could do such a thing, desert your kids, little kids, from two to seven years old? And probably before that, too!

What did you do? Go hole up in a hotel somewhere? What did you do there—lie in a catatonic state for days on end? That's so disgusting; grow up! Maybe we were too demanding and you couldn't handle it. Was your life really that tough? Do you think mine has been any easier? I survived. Why didn't you? Why were you such a destroyer? If you could only feel a little bit of the pain you've caused. What you did has hurt all of us kids, and our kids, our relationships with each other and with other people.

I think you killed Stuart Jr. He was only two and a half years old when you killed yourself. What kind of nurturing did he ever get from you? Right now, I think I'd like to take and pound your face into the pavement for what you've done.

I hate you for what you've done. You and your childish game—holding that knife, threatening Dad and then stabbing yourself. Talk about being the child. How could you do that and leave us all? And say to Dad, "I'm sorry, Stuart; I didn't mean it"? It was too late then.

You know, I've always been glad you died. Faye gets upset with me when I say that, but it's true. You never gave me anything wholesome. You robbed me of my childhood innocence. You never let me be a child. You told me things that made me afraid. You were supposed to make me feel safe. You let me run wild and steal and beat up other kids. What was wrong with you? Why weren't you a mother? I was only five.

What did I ever do to deserve what you did to me? I didn't ask to be born, or to be rejected by you before I even came into the world, to be rejected by you after I arrived, and to be rejected by you when you left me. And not just when you ran away all those times, but when you decided

> *I wasn't important enough for you to stay in this world to help me grow into an adult. Now here I am trying to make sense of my life because of what you did to me.*

Volcano Bubbling Over

The same evening when I was coming to terms with the devastating emotions that surfaced when I read that letter to my therapist, my daughter and I had an argument. That argument had a major influence on both of us for years to come. Tara was fighting for her independence and constantly challenging me. That night, she told me that her friends could all stay out late and she should be able to as well, since it was summer. I told her that it would be hard for me to let her stay out late because I had to get up early for work and wouldn't be able to sleep if she didn't get home at a reasonable time.

She got angry and kept goading me about letting her have her freedom. She was going to be eighteen soon, so she said I would have to let her do what she wanted then. It was a familiar line that she and her dad used repeatedly on me whenever I set boundaries for her. I didn't think the curfew was unrealistic, but she wanted to stretch it out later and later, and I finally drew a line in the sand.

That resulted in us exchanging angry words. I said I thought she should stay with her dad for a few weeks until school started again; he didn't have to get up early for work and I did. I needed a break. The next day, she packed up her things and went to his house.

This was not rejection. It was simply a way for both of us to get through the next two weeks and for me to deal with the emotions that were emerging as I came to terms with the impact of my own mother's death.

When two weeks came and went and school began, I asked Tara when she was coming home.

"I'm not," she said. "You kicked me out."

"I didn't kick you out. I told you it would be good for both of us to take a break."

Most kids from broken homes spend time with both parents, often alternating on holidays and weekends, but I had limited those times as much as I could because of the effect I knew it would have on her to be around her dad. However, I recognized I had to put myself first this time.

I knew Gord's influence on Tara was strong. I think she craved to have him accept her, just as I had during my marriage, when everything I did was wrong in his eyes. I had walked on eggshells around him, hoping they wouldn't break. Over the past eight years, a similar pattern had started to emerge in her. She told me some of the terrible things he said about me. His words were a weapon to hurt her and to hurt me. It never ended. In person, on the phone, when he came to pick her up, when he dropped her off, while she was at his home, he used words to drive nails into both of our hearts.

Tara has been caught most of her life between two parents with very different approaches to parenting and life. That must have torn at her heart; she longed to love and be loved and to accept and be accepted by both of us. It has affected her life and relationships. We continue to struggle from time to time in our mother-daughter relationship because of the multitude of circumstances that have affected us both. As I think of Thelma's illustration of heart wounds, I wonder if the volcano is only quiet on the surface of her life as it hides the reality that it may still be on the verge of bubbling over.

Healing Words and Letting Go

God, my daughter and I went through rocky times for several years. I wanted nothing more than to ensure Tara had all the opportunities I had missed in life. I wanted to be there for her during those significant milestones. I wanted her to talk to me about her boyfriends and to meet them and include them in family activities. I wanted her to ask for my advice about life decisions, such as postsecondary education and marriage. I wanted to attend her graduation and wedding. Instead I missed out on those important milestones with her, as I, at her age, missed out on those times with my own mother.

We both lost something special in our lives because of choices she made. We didn't have that precious mother-daughter bond that becomes even more important when a daughter moves from childhood to adulthood. Tara didn't seem to appreciate the gift of a mother who loved her deeply.

God, I tried to make things better. I ached inside and shed many late-night tears. Our relationship gradually improved, but I put up walls so the pain wouldn't be so intense. What could I have done differently to have the relationship I wanted so badly?

My child, it is not all about you. It is about two people in a relationship wanting something different in life. Your daughter did not experience what you experienced as a child. She took things for granted that you thought she shouldn't. You wanted to ensure your relationship included everything that you didn't have with your mother.

Tara didn't have that need because she had you all those years as she grew up. She felt your love and acceptance, so she was ready to move on to make her own decisions. No, your relationship wasn't perfect and her life hasn't been everything it could be. She could have made other choices in life that would have been better for her and for all those to whom she related.

But life is about learning and growing, and she has done that. Remember the motto she adopted in high school: carpe diem. "Seize the day." Tara has seized the day in her life more than you ever did. She hasn't held tightly to the wounds that could have weighed her down all her life.

Be thankful for that. Be thankful she is as strong as she is. Be thankful she has such a beautiful spirit and energy that people love to be around.

Someday she will realize that aspects of your relationship could have been better. That doesn't mean you cannot have a healthy mother-daughter relationship right now. Just let your past hopes and dreams go and build on what you have, looking forward to the beautiful tomorrows you can share together.

When I started to write that letter to my mother, I had no feelings toward her. Then I felt myself becoming angrier and angrier inside and expressed it in words. I know those feelings resulted from an overwhelming sense of hurt and betrayal. As I read the letter now, I no longer feel anger. Instead, I picture my mother in the arms of God. I picture a woman who must have lived in deep despair for so much of her life. I ache for her pain. Her illness cheated her of a loving relationship with innocent children, a husband who loved her, and the richness that life has to offer.

I realize that I tried to create in my relationship with my own daughter something I didn't need to. It wasn't the relationship I had with my mother. Even as an infant, my daughter must have sensed my love in every word, every smile, and every touch. I encouraged each step she took, literally and figuratively. I tried harder than I needed to and put unnecessary expectations on our relationship. Now it is time to open the door, being confident that it will emerge into something better than it has ever been before.

> *I have found the paradox, that if you love until it hurts, there can be no more hurt, only more love.*
>
> —Mother Teresa[15]

---

15 Mother Teresa, *Brainy Quote*, "Mother Teresa Quotes," January 12, 2014 (http://www.brainyquote.com/quotes/authors/m/mother_teresa.html).

part four

Health

Learning is a gift. Even when pain is your teacher.
—Maya Watson[16]

---

16 Maya Watson, *Twitter*, "Learning is a gift…" July 13, 2012 (https://twitter.com/mayawatson/status/223816183839850499).

chapter six
You Are Clinically Depressed

Have you gone through all of this for nothing? Is it all really for nothing?

—Galatians 3:4 (CEV)

SUICIDAL CRISIS

Many people think that someone with a depressive disorder who talks about suicide is destined to take his or her life someday. Many attempt it; many succeed. Others are on the cusp while some still play with the possibility, and still others cry out for help. I learned that what they are experiencing is called a suicidal crisis. People can often get through that crisis just like other difficulties if they have the right supports in place.

I've connected with many people online who shared their pain in the cyber world. I often wonder why it seems so much easier to reveal to strangers that you're depressed and planning to drive your car off the road, take pills, jump off a bridge, or attempt any number of other means of ending your life. Why not tell people you know, people nearby who can help you through the crisis? I wonder how much the desire for anonymity results because of the stigma of mental illness.

Most of the people I initially connected with were young women, from eighteen years old into their mid-twenties, whom I met on social media sites. Increasingly, I have come across online comments by middle-aged men and women about their plans to end their lives because of the despair they feel, often during a time of marriage breakdown or unemployment. I have tried to encourage them by sharing my own family's experiences and the heartbreak that suicide brought, and by making them aware of useful online resources and inspirational materials.

I discovered one website that houses an insightful article called "If You Are Thinking About Suicide… Read This First." Accompanying the text is an image of a balance scale with the words "pain" and "coping resources" on each side. What struck me most was this statement: "Suicide is not chosen; it happens when pain exceeds resources for coping with pain."[17] To bring us back into balance, we need to balance the scale.

How do people rebalance the scale? Sometimes it's simply asking for emotional support from others who care. At other times, it comes from someone recognizing another person's struggles and offering unsolicited help. Medication is often used, typically as an intervention for people who are clinically depressed. Counseling and other medical and psychological interventions also come into play. Sometimes people are so severely depressed that they require hospitalization with intensive therapy to get them through the

---

17 *Metanoia*, "If You Are Thinking About Suicide… Read This First," December 22, 2013 (http://www.metanoia.org/suicide/).

most difficult phase. I wonder if it would have made a difference for my mother and brother if this kind of information had been readily available to them.

Major Depressive Disorder

My personal introduction to a major depressive episode was a disturbing experience, especially for someone as independent as me—someone who doesn't like relying on others for support. My husband and I had separated earlier that year. I wonder at times if our separation and the ensuing events triggered my depression, or if it would have happened regardless of what I was going through.

Two months before a full-blown depressive episode hit, I quit my job as the director of an out-of-school care program. I had deep concerns because the owner's lack of integrity and disregard for government standards could have affected my own professional reputation. The day I resigned is the same day that a major financial institution holding a small amount of savings in my name suddenly declared bankruptcy. That money was all I had to sustain myself and pay my bills. A series of problems emerged with my house and vehicle that required money, and I had little money. My short-term alimony and limited child support funds didn't even cover my mortgage, let alone any other expenses.

I was homeschooling my daughter at the time and trying to figure out the easiest way to transition her into school with the least negative effect. I had a homeschoolers meeting at my house one night. We had just formed a new provincial home education association and I had been elected vice-president. Usually, I was very articulate and passionate, as I had a burning desire to create support systems for parents who wanted to homeschool their children. So many people I encountered didn't believe in themselves. "You can do it," they would say. "You're a teacher. But what about me?" The supports I helped provide, such as homeschooling resources and parent groups, helped renew the parents' belief in themselves; they knew what was best for their children and could homeschool successfully.

It was also an opportunity to continue the education they had begun with their children the moment they were born, and in some cases even before they were born. Research tells us that talking, singing, and reading to our children in the womb have positive effects on their growth and development.

That night, I was not my typical self. I didn't exude my usual enthusiasm. I couldn't speak in the normally informed manner that made others feel both comfortable and reassured. I didn't lead discussions, with others looking to me for answers. Instead, I was strangely quiet. I sat at the dining room table with the rest of the group and felt jitters inside my head. I couldn't think clearly. I was in a fog. I fought back the tears hidden just beneath the surface of my eyelids, my tear ducts trying to release them, my inner resistance holding them back.

What Can I Do to Help You?

When the meeting was over, I was so exhausted that I wanted to go to bed. I was afraid of the feelings threatening to expose me as someone I didn't want to be, someone I perceived as weak. One close homeschooling friend, Sandy, stayed behind and we moved into the living room.

How I wished she would leave. But she stayed. She chatted about the meeting and other things while I tried to contain myself, ready to collapse physically and emotionally. She finally said the words that were on her heart.

"There's something wrong with you. What is it? I could see how different you were in the meeting tonight. What can I do to help you?"

What could she do to help me? I had difficulty processing that question. It had always been about what I could do to help others. Maybe it wasn't just that I wanted to help others, but that I wouldn't allow others to help me. I opened myself to that realization as time ticked by. The dam finally broke and my fragmented thoughts poured out as words:

"I don't know what's wrong with me. I'm scared. I don't like the way I'm thinking. I think about the same things over and over and can't stop. I feel like my head is a TV screen full of snow. I feel cold and numb all through my body. I don't sleep. I don't want to eat. I feel like I can't function. I feel guilty that I'm not there for my daughter. I'm afraid because I haven't found a job and I'm running out of money. I don't know if I should sell the house or try to keep it so Tara has a place she feels safe. I don't want her to go through the turmoil I went through in my life with moving every year, never having friends, and feeling like I didn't belong. At the employment office the other day, they told me I'm doing everything right so I should just keep trying. I became really emotional and tearful there. I feel so useless and incompetent. It seems like the tears keep coming and I can't stop them and I don't like it. I know I need to see a doctor, but I don't know what to do."

Sandy told me I definitely needed to see a doctor. She could see the difference in me from the last time we had been together. She talked gently, supporting and encouraging me. She made me feel reassured for those few hours we talked. It was after 2:30 a.m. before she finally left, saying she was going to contact me the next day with some ideas on how to get help.

I sank into bed, not fully appreciating the lifeline she had given me. My pain had been out of balance with my coping resources. Sandy had just tipped the scale back a little, so I wouldn't collapse under the weight of pain pulling me down.

Introduction to the Mental Health System

The next morning, I couldn't get out of bed. I just lay there, feeling like heavy bricks were piled on top of me. Tara, the most precious gift in the world to me, came into my room. I said I wasn't feeling well, so she went downstairs and made herself something to eat and brought something up for me.

Sandy called in the late morning and said she was going to pick me up and take me to the walk-in psychiatric clinic at the university hospital. I had no idea what a walk-in clinic was, but I had let go by this time. I allowed her to do what she needed to do for me. We couldn't have lived any further apart, but she drove across the city to take me there, inconvenient though it was. Her hands were full with her own two homeschooling daughters, and her third child was on the way.

She brought me to the walk-in clinic just as it opened for afternoon intakes, then took my daughter to spend time with her children. The desk clerk gave me a long questionnaire to fill in. She told me that people saw a psychiatrist on a priority basis, determined by an assessment of their individual situation, and there was no guarantee anyone would see me that day.

I sat down and attempted to fill in the form. It was a struggle. The questions didn't make sense to my fuzzy brain. It felt like I was short-circuiting continually, as if my brain were a frayed wire plugged into an electrical outlet. I still experienced cold and numbness throughout my body. Strange sensations passed through me and strange chemicals seemed to flow through my veins, feeling like poison.

Eventually, I did complete the form and handed it back to the desk clerk. Then I waited. As the clinic hours ticked by, I thought the clerk would tell me to go home and come back another day. I hoped not. It was Friday and the weekend was coming. I could already feel it was going to be a weekend of terror for me, with my fears increasing minute by minute. Finally, the clerk called me to her desk and told me that a psychiatrist would see me shortly. A female assistant came and ushered me into the doctor's office. I don't remember his name; I do remember him scrutinizing the form I had filled in.

He asked me questions; I have no idea what they were or how many he asked. Most of the session was a blur, but I clearly remember the words he spoke near the end: "You are clinically depressed. You are experiencing a major depression." I didn't know what he meant. How could that be? My own mother and younger brother had taken their own lives and my older brother had attempted suicide several times already, but I still didn't understand the meaning of the doctor's words.

When I think of it, I want to go back and change things. I want to shake myself and ask why. Why didn't I learn more about depression? Why didn't I try to figure out what happened to my younger brother? I had concluded that he took his life because of a series of difficult situations he was facing at the time that were too much for him—his marriage breakdown, the loss of his job, and the looming loss of his home.

I had told people during that early grieving time that if only he had hung on until springtime, he would have warmed up inside just as the sun's rays warmed the earth. I had believed it because I've experienced seasonal affective disorder every winter since I was a young adult. Every year, I count the days until the spring sunshine floods in to erase the darkness of the winter months.

So there I was, facing a diagnosis of clinical depression, not really comprehending what it meant. Looking back now, this seems so strange because I typically want to understand everything that doesn't make sense.

Maybe if there had been an Internet back then, I would have researched mental health topics. The Internet has provided a wealth of information and has opened up a world of people who want to share their personal experiences. That is a good thing. I hope that over time the stigma of mood disorders, including depressive illness, is dispelled or minimized.

Hoping for a Quick Fix

The next few months were rocky ones. With a prescription in hand and future appointments booked at the walk-in clinic, I was ready for a cure. Being a task-oriented person, I anticipated getting the

Chapter Six: You Are Clinically Depressed • 83

job done quickly. I had the knowledge (at least, I had one book on symptoms related to mental health disorders). I had the medication, which the doctor said I needed to treat the extensive symptoms affecting my brain and permeating every fiber of my being. I was going to see someone for a follow-up appointment so I could gather more information, which would contribute to my arsenal. Knowledge is power; I would have power again and not feel so weak and vulnerable.

Things didn't go as well as I had expected. The day after seeing the psychiatrist, I felt worse. Somehow I assumed that a dose or two of medication would have an immediate positive effect, but it didn't. One of my younger sisters, Debbie, phoned and could tell by my voice that something was seriously wrong. She told my dad.

When Dad got on the phone, I told him that I was just feeling a bit overwhelmed with everything, looking for a job and dealing with household issues. I had a leak in my shower and didn't have money to get it fixed. So Dad and my youngest brother, Bruce, came over, regrouted the tiles on the walls surrounding the shower, and sealed the edges with silicone.

We never discussed what was really going on. I thought Dad shouldn't have to hear about another of his children dealing with depression, so I kept silent. It took another three months before I managed to sponge down and seal the grout for the bathroom tiles. It's a good thing we had more than one shower.

And the medication… I went through several different medications, because they didn't seem to help. They always felt like poison to my system and caused serious side effects. Besides my visits to psychiatrists, I also saw my family doctor. I talked to him about the panic attacks I was experiencing and how I had to breathe into a brown paper bag that I carried everywhere. On one visit, my hands were shaking so badly, and my body was so full of jitters, that he prescribed a tranquilizer. For some reason, I had a bad feeling about trying it.

That night, I was talking to a friend's sister, who was a psychiatric nurse. I told her about my fear of medicating myself with yet another drug. She said I should take it because the doctor had prescribed it and he obviously knew what he was doing. I asked her to stay on the phone while I took one pill. She agreed, so I took it and we kept talking.

Thirty to forty-five minutes later, I became hysterical, laughing and crying, hyperventilating, then going into a panic attack—terrified of what was happening. She talked me down and suggested I don't take any more of the pills.

When I went to my doctor the next day, he told me that I had experienced a paradoxical reaction, the opposite to how a person should respond to that type of medication. I wonder now, with all the antidepressant medications I have tried over the years and the negative side effects that resulted, if it was because depression wasn't my real condition.

Up and Down

A friend, Pam, called me late one evening to see how I was doing. She was one of only a handful of friends to whom I confided about what was happening. I felt I had a responsibility to educate at least a few people about depression. I told Pam that I was afraid. I had been going in overdrive all day. I couldn't slow down. My mind was flying in a million directions. I didn't know why I suddenly changed from my lethargic state to feeling like I had superpowers. I felt I could do anything, accomplish anything, and that I didn't need any sleep. Then I felt like I was falling apart; inside my head, it was like a TV screen out of focus. I was shaky all over. I was agitated, scared, and cold.

Pam cautioned me to slow down and get some rest. These were wise words, but I simply ignored them. I stayed up most of the night, accomplishing so much that I hadn't been able to do only a few days before. I don't know how I missed cleaning the bathroom tiles that night. Everything else was spotless.

This didn't last long, as I soon crashed down into a deep and overwhelming depression. That cycle of ups and downs went on for the next year as I applied for jobs and got interview appointments, but then had to turn them down because I didn't have enough energy to go. Or worse yet, I went anyway and was unable to convince the interview panel I was the right person for the job because of how I felt at the time.

I spent my meager savings foolishly. First, I bought a whole line of educational toys and became an educational toy consultant. I had no real return on investment for my intermittent work in this area. Then, with my remaining funds, I purchased a high-end vacuum cleaner and had a short-lived sporadic career as a vacuum salesperson. My depressive state didn't give me the capacity to effectively present the value of educational toys or vacuum cleaners to those who agreed to attend my demonstrations.

Strangely, the medical profession didn't recognize or diagnose the meaning of these cycles as they continually adjusted the medications designed to treat me for depression.

Moving through the System

My psychiatrist, after his initial triage approach, referred me to another psychiatrist shortly after my first visit. As I sat in the second psychiatrist's waiting room, I stared at an abstract art piece on the wall. If I had been asked to give it a name, I would have called it "Chaos." It had no pattern, with lines going in all directions, with blue and yellow blobs of color.

I told the psychiatrist when I went into his office that I thought they put up pictures like that on purpose to make people think they were crazy.

"Have you been having any hallucinations lately?" he asked.

"No," I said, "other than the afternoon I lay in bed and heard voices downstairs when I was all alone and then saw tiny motorcycles flying in and out of my ears with little people on them… if you call that hallucinations."

He must have thought it was a joke and decided I had stabilized enough to refer me for weekly visits to a counselor. Her name was Jean.

During the first counseling visit, I shed some tears and didn't like it. Jean was at least ten years younger than me and likely a new graduate of a Master's program in counselling. She thought she knew all about me from reading my file and talking briefly with me. When I told her some of my experiences, she came to a rapid conclusion about my problems.

"You have had a lot of losses in your life, and you haven't dealt with them," she said. "You lost your mother, you lost your brother, and you lost your marriage. That's why you're depressed."

"No, I don't think that's the issue at all," I bluntly replied. "I know I've had a lot of losses, but I think I've dealt with them just fine."

"I think you like to be in control," Jean said, surprising me.

"Well, if that were true, my husband wouldn't have walked all over me. He was the controller, not me."

Jean sighed. "I don't think you recognize, or want to admit, that you need help."

"I have reached out," I said pointedly. "I know that I'm depressed. I just don't know if the treatments are working. My moods go up and down. I'm just trying to make sense of things. I wonder, if an antidepressant is designed to bring a person out of a low state, could it overcompensate and take a person too high?"

Sometimes I have a way of intimidating people by speaking frankly about my perceptions and beliefs.

That's what happened at our next appointment. Shortly after the session began, I calmly asked Jean why she was so angry. I could see it in her face, hear it in her voice, and feel it spread throughout the room, casting its rays outward to land on me.

That stopped her short. Her mannerisms, toughness, and facial expressions softened. I noticed the wrinkles around her eyes for the first time. *She's older than I thought*, I said to myself. Before, she had seemed so much younger than me.

I wondered if the issue between Jean and me was that we both had preset agendas for our time together, but neither of us could accomplish what we wanted because we threw each other off-track, her wanting the conversation to go in one direction and me wanting it to go down another path.

On the third of our sessions, Jean told me that she had talked to the psychiatrist in charge and they had both decided that I needed to be in "group."

"I don't want to be in group, whatever that is," I responded. "I connect better with people on a one-on-one basis."

"We know," Jean said. "That's why you need to be in group."

Group

The next week, I went to group. Jean had made "group" sound like a dirty word. Two facilitators, Rob and Lorraine, sat waiting for me as I walked into the room. There were no introductions. I sat down in a circle of people who had mostly been attending previously. I waited for the counselors to introduce me, introduce the topic, and start discussing issues. Instead, all they did was sit quietly, until one of them finally asked, "Who wants to talk first?"

Talk first? Talk about what? What a weird approach to counseling this was. I had participated in personal growth and marriage counseling and went through my most recent foray into individual counseling for depression. But what was this process? Where was the structure? Weren't people supposed to take turns talking about their problems, with others contributing their solutions? I was good at those types of discussions. I attended many meetings at work where we did extensive problem solving.

The only worthwhile part of the program for the first several weeks was the intrigue of this technique. I kept observing, trying to figure out what was really going on.

But then something happened at home that increased my negative perception of the group process. I had a very strange experience that I felt compelled to write down. I came to a new understanding about why some people take their own lives, a very different perspective from the usual sense-of-hopelessness view people often describe.

From the time I received my clinical depression diagnosis, I had been trying to make sense of why people killed themselves. I needed to understand it for myself, and for my mother and brother. In the early days of my illness, I hadn't felt like killing myself and I couldn't understand why my brother had done it. This is what I wrote:

> *I think that people who do it must, at some point, get a strong overpowering urge that is beyond reason and control. I thought I understood the reasons for it before—people feeling depressed and believing that there is no hope for the future.*
>
> *I'm not so sure now that is really what they feel. This sense I am getting now about the whole thing puts my thinking in a different perspective. I just keep blocking it out, because I feel afraid of the power that motivates suicide.*
>
> *I think that people who are left behind always try to analyze what caused it. They can't understand, just as I couldn't understand when my brother did it. I tried to figure out what went on in his mind, just as other people did, but none of us had experienced that power, that driving force, that compulsion.*
>
> *It may be something like the urge that some people have to jump when they are standing on a bridge looking down. Something seems to pull, to draw them into the*

> *depths. So whether it is the water that draws, or the compulsion to overdose on pills, or the desire to gas oneself or shoot oneself, it is almost a fascination, a hypnotizing force.*

The next week at group, I walked in a few minutes early with those words on a paper. Lorraine was there, but Rob was out of town. I told Lorraine that I had something to share with her, which I thought might give her new insights into why people took their own lives. She told me she wouldn't read it.

"Share it with the group," she said.

"But I want to share it with you," I replied.

She shook her head and said nothing. I walked to my chair and sat there for the session, anger building inside me. I didn't speak during that very long afternoon.

I returned the next week, still angry. When Rob asked who wanted to share first, I spoke up.

"I *am* angry about the group process," I said in a firm and deliberate voice. "None of it makes sense. You never gave us any rules, but when someone breaks an unspoken rule, you let us know. That's what happened to me last week. Neither of you ever told us we couldn't share something with you privately, but when I did, Lorraine made me feel foolish for breaking a rule that I hadn't even known existed. What are we doing here, anyway? All you do is sit and wait for people to talk.

"It really annoys me that you talk about us before and after the session. I'd like to be in your meeting room, listening to those discussions. I'd like to know what you're planning and what you're saying about me. I'd like to hear whether you think I've made any progress.

"I really dislike the fact that this is such a fluid group. People keep coming and going from week to week, and there are no introductions or goodbyes. We can't bond as a group because we don't know who's going to be here next week or why someone stops coming. I would never do that to anyone. If I decided not to come back, I would make sure to come one last time to say goodbye. After all, that's the respectful thing to do."

I smile now as I recall that day. I think Lorraine and Rob must have had a productive debriefing after it was over, pleased to see that I had finally opened up and expressed my feelings. I had held things in for so long. I hadn't really been part of the group. I was an outsider looking in, advising other participants on their pain. I told them why people treated them the way they did and what they could do differently to resolve their issues.

At one session, a woman tried to make sense of what was going on in her relationship with her husband. She cried openly and I told her that I knew why she was feeling the way she was—her husband was treating her with disrespect. I pointed to the floor and stated in a composed manner, "That is your head on the floor. You know what he's doing? He's grinding your head into the floor." I lifted my feet and then drove them into the floor with great force. "He's abusing you." Only later did I realize that I was illustrating in this way to the group what I had experienced in my own marriage.

When I finally began to show emotion in the group, I decided it was time to stop attending the weekly sessions. That afternoon, while others talked, I felt myself crying silently deep within my inner being. The tremendous pain would not stay inside, so the tears began running down my cheeks and my body started to heave quietly. I didn't want anyone to notice, but Lorraine finally said, "Does anyone notice anything about Bonnie?"

All eyes turned on me now. I was no longer the problem solver for other people's pain. I was vulnerable, just as they were, showing emotions that made me feel small and weak. I couldn't explain my pain, my tears, my overwhelming feelings.

Was I beginning to deal with heart wounds so deep that they weren't yet able to surface? I decided that this process wasn't working for me anymore. I came back the next week and told everyone that I didn't feel there was any value in me continuing to attend; I had attended for six months and made no progress. This would be my last day. I just was not ready to let go of the pain.

The Ongoing Battle

This was not the end of my battle. It took over a year before I was able to work; I tried different medications under constant supervision of my doctor.

Several times that year, I sat crying in my garage, silently acknowledging to myself that I could now comprehend why Stuart Jr. had ended his life. I experienced the feeling that life would never get better. I felt the bleakness, the hopelessness, and the pain that doesn't end. Leaving the car running would make it all go away.

I finally understood why my mother had taken her own life and left her children behind. I loved my own daughter more than I could describe, and it broke my heart to think of ever hurting her. Even so, I knew that love wasn't strong enough to hold me back when my illness entrenched suicidal thoughts that wouldn't let go, when the power drew me in and the blackness was just too black.

That was a sad realization. I prayed many times for God to take away my thoughts of ending it all.

I have memories of a day, early on, when Tara brought me a bookmark with a poem titled "Don't Quit." I kept it in my Bible, read it every day, and in my tearful state cried out to God to help me internalize those words and spare my life so her heart wouldn't be broken. I didn't want Tara to go through life without a mother, as I had done. Mercifully, he pulled me back from the brink more than once.

For the next year, I still went through times when I wondered if I would ever be well again.

> *That's the thing about depression: A human being can survive almost anything, as long as she sees the end in sight. But depression is so insidious… that it's impossible to ever see the end. The fog is like a cage without a key.*
> —Elizabeth Wurtzel[18]

Thankfully, I gradually recovered. I began to rebuild my health, my hope for the future, and my career.

HEALING WORDS AND LETTING GO

God, what is the lesson in this experience? I have always wanted to be strong and independent, not leaning on others. Instead of running away when I finally got to the point of vulnerability in the

---

18 Elizabeth Wurtzel, *Prozac Nation* (New York, NY: Berkley Publishing Group, 1994), 191.

group, maybe my healing would have happened sooner if I had let others help me.

My child, you fought a hard fight, especially in that first year of your illness. You, the strong one, the one to whom your brother turned, asking you to help the family over his death. You, who hid your pain. You, who needed to walk through the valley yourself, the valley of hopelessness and despair. You needed to feel, not think. You needed to know that there are no easy answers to offer for those dealing with depression.

You always resented your mother. You said you were glad she died because she wasn't a mother to you. She fought such a battle. She didn't have the resources back in those days that you had. You had a friend who pointed you in the right direction to get help. You had friends who checked in on you and listened, even when they couldn't understand. You had medical doctors, counselors, and medication to get you through the crises.

You could have used the group more effectively, not only to serve their needs, but also to be ministered to by them. I planted people in that group who could relate to your pain, which was different but the same. Pain is pain, tears are tears, and a wounded heart is wounded. I wanted to use those individuals to bring you to a better place so you could heal sooner, but you didn't accept my gift.

So many times in life, you haven't allowed yourself to live with joy because you wanted to do things on your own. You didn't allow others, those I provided as a support system, to help you. You cry out to me and ask for my help. Don't you see? It is so important for the hearts of humankind to connect with the hearts of others. Although I am ever-present, I still created you to need each other, to need words and looks of encouragement, to feel love from the hugs of people who could warm your soul.

That balance scale you wrote about earlier—pain versus coping resources—I have filled this world with coping resources. Now you know what some of them are. You know the feelings of desperation, isolation, and blackness. You can use your experiences to help others who are struggling. You can point them to what you have gone through in your life, and to the coping resources you have found to support you. You can help them understand how to survive the pain.

> *God… comforts us in all our troubles, so that we can comfort those in any trouble with the comfort we ourselves receive from God.*
>
> —2 Corinthians 1:3–4

Release your pain. Let it go. Be a friend. I have given you a sensitive spirit, a radar that zooms in on hurting hearts that need to heal. That radar is a gift. Your health challenges are a gift, and your losses are a gift, all gifts given from my heart.

I always thought that independence was a good thing. I had to be independent from a young age because of my circumstances, but life provides a mixture of dependence, independence, and interdependence. God has given us all three as ways of living and relating with others and with him.

I see now that interdependence is as important as independence. I have difficulty allowing people to help me, but I find it easy to help others. When I don't let others support me, I deny them the privilege of giving the gift of themselves.

God, just as interdependence is critical to forming and maintaining relationships with others, dependence is vital to a healthy relationship with you. When I don't rely on you, I am in essence rejecting all that you are—a God of indescribable love!

> *How great is the love the Father has given us so freely! Now we can be called children of God. And that's what we really are!*
>
> —1 John 3:1 (NIrV)

> *If you can believe the God who is perfect loves you, then you can believe that you are worth loving.*
>
> —Joyce Meyer[19]

---

19 Joyce Meyer, *Beauty for Ashes: Receiving Emotional Healing* (New York, NY: Warner Books, 2003), 194.

chapter seven
I'm Not Depressed, I'm Just Tired

Bipolar disorder can be a great teacher. It's a challenge, but it can set you up to be able to do almost anything else in your life.

—Carrie Fisher [20]

I NEED PAINT

Sixteen years after my severe clinical depressive episode, I found myself experiencing intense exhaustion. An incident occurred at work with my supervisor that really upset me and I could hardly get out of bed the next day. I called in sick. I was barely able to walk to the refrigerator or the bathroom to take care of my basic needs. When people called me on the phone, it took all my strength to speak loudly enough for them to hear me. Those extreme symptoms continued for over three weeks as I spent most of my time in bed.

---

20 Carrie Fisher, *iCelebZ*, "Carrie Fisher Quotes/Quotations," December 23, 2013 (http://www.icelebz.com/quotes/carrie_fisher/).

Then I suddenly became energized. I decided I needed paint for the new doors in the house and the trim on the house exterior. On a sunny fall day, I went to the paint store and came back with various paint cans.

I spent the next several days painting everything in sight. I half-finished painting the kitchen cupboards, then ran out of energy and quit. For months, I had to look at those unsightly cupboards, half of them a creamy ivory color and the remaining ones still a tasteless spackled blue.

Over a number of weeks, I fluctuated between total collapse and excessive levels of energy. My doctor focused on the symptoms of exhaustion and told me I was depressed. I told him I wasn't depressed. I didn't feel like crying and wasn't thinking negative thoughts. I didn't ruminate or manifest the symptoms I had experienced when I'd previously been diagnosed with depression. I just felt extreme fatigue in every fiber of my body. The doctor prescribed an antidepressant that cost $150 a month, and I had no drug plan at the time to reduce the cost.

Soon after starting the medication, I spent one of my good days with a friend checking out real estate in a small town not far from home. On the way back that afternoon, we stopped at a restaurant for tea. My eyes started to blur over and I felt very dizzy. I thought I was going to pass out, and I knew it was because of the drugs. The drugs always made me feel that way, like some kind of poison was spreading through me.

We left the restaurant. By the time I got home, I discovered I had broken out in a rash that covered my chest. I went to my doctor the next day and he told me to stop taking the drugs. I still had over $120 worth left. I wish I could have returned the remaining pills as

I often return things to Walmart, no questions asked. I would have used the money to buy more paint.

Facing Reality

I had been off work for about two months. A nurse from my workplace's employee support program contacted me, asking about my personal and family medical history. I told her that my mother had died by suicide when I was young. I explained that we never knew exactly what was wrong with her, but she'd had a history of mental health issues.

I also told her about my younger brother's death—that he had never demonstrated any signs of depression before, but that he likely had a depressive episode resulting from the significant losses in his life in the months preceding his death. I also told her about all the challenges my older brother had experienced since his early twenties, with several conflicting diagnoses of schizophrenia and bipolar disorder.

I finally volunteered that I suspected I had bipolar disorder. I thought back on my whole adult life and could recall behavior patterns that seemed to reflect that diagnosis, but they were not as incapacitating as during my major depressive episode years earlier, or even at this point in my life.

My writings from my early twenties often revealed my struggles and questions, although I didn't clearly articulate my concerns. At times I felt like I was flying high, and then I would come crashing down. None of those cycles lasted for extended periods, however, or caused noticeable issues with my interpersonal relationships or employment.

This was the first time I had voiced my suspicions aloud to anyone. I had never wanted to face the possibility that I might be right. My first major depressive episode, though, had been almost more than I could deal with. At that time, I told a close home-schooling friend, Lynne, that I might write a book about it someday.

I saw the ignorance of so many people regarding mental health issues and wanted to provide an education on what it was like. I wanted to open people's eyes to the reality that there should be no shame, no stigma regarding mental illness. I have said a hundred times over the years that we don't judge people with physical disorders such as cancer, heart disease, or diabetes, but when we find out that someone has a mental health disorder, we immediately pass judgment or tell jokes.

I went to see a psychiatrist who confirmed my self-diagnosis of bipolar disorder. He thanked my family doctor for referring this "interesting lady" to him. He recommended that I take lithium. It took almost three months before I decided to get the prescription filled and take the medication, and it took considerably more time for my body to adjust to it. I felt like I was walking around in slow motion for weeks, but for the first time in my adult life, my brain actually shut off and I slept soundly through the night without a million thoughts and ideas racing through my mind.

Finally, some of the events and activities of my life began to make sense, such as why I could seldom go to sleep at night like other people, and how I once operated on less than two hours of sleep a night for four months until I finally ran out of energy. I accomplished so much during that time. I typically got a power boost at around 11:00 p.m., when I should have been going to sleep. To make the most of it, I signed up for numerous courses, thinking I might as well do something useful. One day, I counted the books on my bed and beside my bed; there were over thirty, all at some stage of being read.

I recalled the year when I decided to be an investor, just before the tech wreck of 2000. I invested heavily in stocks and other funds that I thought made sense at the time, but in retrospect I realize they did not. One day, I went into church laughing because I had just lost several thousand dollars on paper the day before. One of my friends was shocked, asking why I wasn't upset. It was an adrenal rush and a fascinating game to me. I stopped looking at the numbers after a while because the paper losses translated to real losses and kept climbing. I realized that retirement would be further away than I had anticipated. Much further away!

THE STIGMA AND THE SHAME

> *Mental illness is nothing to be ashamed of, but stigma and bias shame us all.*
>
> —Bill Clinton[21]

After my clinical depression diagnosis, I tried to get others to understand that depression and other mood disorders are legitimate illnesses. If someone is ill, that doesn't warrant snide remarks and cruel jokes. It is appalling how many people I know have made insensitive comments about depression, bipolar disorder, and schizophrenia, labels they could put on me and on other family members if they knew our circumstances. I've usually said nothing,

---

21 William Clinton, *The American Presidency Project*, "William J. Clinton," December 23, 2013 (http://www.presidency.ucsb.edu/ws/index.php?pid=57689).

afraid that revealing my own situation could affect both my personal and professional relationships.

Statistics tell us that almost ten percent of the United States' adult population has a mood disorder—a major depressive disorder, dysthmic disorder (chronic mild depression), or bipolar disorder.[22] Most people must have encountered a family member, friend, or colleague with this type of health issue. Sometimes it can be debilitating, but often it is not, particularly when people are under a doctor's care. Why then are there so many negative perceptions? Why do people still make assumptions about a person's ability to do a job, take care of a family, and have functional relationships? Why don't we support those who struggle instead of sentencing them to a life of isolation and alienation?

People have to be so careful about sharing their stories. Even I, who have lived and breathed mental illness with other family members and in person, have been reluctant to share about it in the workplace. I've feared that other staff would measure everything I did against the stereotype of the words "mental illness."

If interpersonal relationship difficulties were to occur, I would likely be pointed to as the one at fault because of my illness. Only recently, as I came closer to retiring, did I begin to open up to some staff about my challenges, mainly in conversations about publishing this book.

Even with family members who should know better, the blame and shame is often there. I recently encountered an interpersonal situation in my own family where the fault was placed entirely on

---

22 U.S. Department of Health and Human Services, *National Institute of Health*, "Mood Disorders," December 23, 2013 (http://report.nih.gov/NIHfactsheets/ViewFactSheet.aspx?csid=48).

me. More than one family member was responsible for the problem, but my disorder suddenly became the cause of everything that had transpired. In truth, it had nothing to do with the situation. The issue was simply poor communication between the parties involved.

Society as a whole does not understand mental illness and is uneducated on the range of symptoms and forms it can take. The judgment and double standards continue. What if we took the word "mental" out of mental illness and just said that a person had an illness? Would that make any difference in people's perceptions and in reducing the stigma?

Fortunately, my experience with mood disorders has been beneficial in many ways. For most of my career, I've been able to do the job of two or three people, and others are amazed at what I can accomplish. I just tell them that I'm like the Energizer Bunny; I keep going and going and going.

In my thirty-year career, I missed one year of work while dealing with my first diagnosis of severe depressive illness, shortly after my marriage separation. Since then, I missed four months of work during the time I received a bipolar disorder diagnosis. I take a low dose of medication daily. Although I have experienced many episodes of both depression and mania, I have managed them with medication, education and other supports, so they've had limited impact on my overall functioning.

I've worked hard and have an excellent work ethic. Everything I've done has been to the standard of perfection. I've received numerous awards and superior performance ratings. I never wanted to climb the workplace ladder; I just wanted to do a good job wherever I was. In spite of that, supervisors kept recognizing my skills and offering me new opportunities.

On this basis, can people say my illness is debilitating? I don't think so. But how would it be interpreted if my employer read my story? What would it say to those people at my church who have said adamantly that anyone with this type of problem simply lacks faith and that they should be able to pray it away?

> *... neither height[s] nor depth[s ...] will be able to separate us from the love of God that is in Christ Jesus our Lord.*
> —Romans 8:39

It's Not Rare, It's Everywhere

Not everyone has been as fortunate as me. Many, like my older brother, experience such extreme mood disorders that they don't make good treatment choices, such as regularly taking medications that have positive effects. Almost forty percent of homeless people in North America report some kind of mental illness problems,[23] yet mainstream society shuns them and labels them as alcoholics and drug addicts. That attitude is a great tragedy, both for the individuals who need help and for society as a whole.

I discovered that I am in good company with numerous well-known authors diagnosed with bipolar disorder, including Ernest Hemingway, Robert Munsch, and Virginia Woolf. Kay Redfield Jamison, a clinical psychologist and author who has personally experienced bipolar disorder, has written extensively on the subject. In her book *Night Falls Fast*, Ms. Jamison writes, "Every seventeen

---

23 Public Broadcasting Service, *PBS.org*, "Facts and Figures: The Homeless," December 23, 2013 (http://www.pbs.org/now/shows/526/homeless-facts.html).

minutes in America, someone commits suicide… I have been impressed by how little value our society puts on saving the lives of those who are in such despair as to want to end them. It is a societal illusion that suicide is rare. It is not."[24]

I learned that suicide is the fourth leading cause of death in the United States for people ages eighteen to sixty-five—to me, a surprising statistic.[25] Also, "of the 4,000 Canadians who die every year as a result of suicide, most were confronting a mental health problem or illness."[26]

Prominent individuals from different occupations and lifestyles carry the bipolar label, including Winston Churchill, one of the world's greatest political leaders of all time, who struggled with his "black dog."

I don't like standing near the edge of a platform when an express train is passing through. I like to stand right back and if possible get a pillar between me and the train. I don't like to stand by the side of a ship and look down into the water. A second's action would end everything.

—Winston Churchill[27]

---

24 Kay Redfield Jamison, *Night Falls Fast: Understanding Suicide* (New York, NY: Alfred A. Knopf, 1999), 309–310.

25 U.S. Department of Health and Human Services, *National Institute of Mental Health*, "Leading Causes of Death Ages 18–65 in the U.S.," December 23, 2013 (http://www.nimh.nih.gov/statistics/3AGES1865.shtml). Chart created in 2007.

26 *Changing Directions, Changing Lives: The Mental Health Strategy of Canada* (Ottawa, ON: Mental Health Commission of Canada, 2012), 19. Available at http://strategy.mentalhealthcommission.ca/pdf/strategy-images-en.pdf.

27 Winston Churchill, *Bipolar Lives*, "Bipolar and Suicide…" December 23, 2013 (http://www.bipolar-lives.com/quotes-on-bipolar.html).

After the 2012 school shooting tragedy in Newtown, Connecticut, Patrick Kennedy, a former United States senator, openly spoke of his bipolar disorder. He has played, and continues to play, a key role in breaking down the pervasive stigma associated with mental illness. Upon leaving Congress and moving into the next chapter in his life as a private citizen, he has made the pursuit of mental health parity a key priority.

BLACK HALO

It is during our darkest moments that we must focus to see the light.

—Aristotle Onassis[28]

One year, my supervisor learned of my challenges. I had lived for seven years symptom-free of any lingering effects from my first major depressive episode. Then, one Saturday night when my daughter was at a friend's house for the weekend, a powerful urge came over me, similar to that overwhelming force I had wanted to share with my counselor in the group session.

I wanted to go into the garage and turn on the car and let it run. No one would have found me because Tara wouldn't have gotten home until late the next day. I didn't feel depressed, sad, or angry. I wasn't losing weight or gaining weight. I wasn't ruminating, fixating, or having difficulty sleeping. What was going on?

---

28 Aristotle Onassis, *Brainy Quote*, "Aristotle Onassis Quotes," January 25, 2014 (http://www.brainyquote.com/quotes/authors/a/aristotle_onassis.html).

I somehow survived the night and the next day, begging God to keep me from taking that death walk. On Monday afternoon, my supervisor came into my office and talked to me. I didn't sense anything different about our chat, but he began a circuitous conversation that eventually led to this question: "What is going on with you?"

My responses, one after another, didn't satisfy him. "I'm not sure I want to do this job anymore. I'm looking for something more interesting, more challenging. It's frustrating and I don't feel I'm contributing in any significant way. I wonder if my life would have more meaning if I had a different job."

At the end of each statement, he said, "No, that's not it. I know there's something more."

Finally, exhausted, irritated, and at the end of excuses, I said, "Do you really want to know what's going on? I want to kill myself and I don't know why. I'm scared. I made an appointment with my doctor. I don't know what to do."

"I could tell it was something serious," he said. "I saw the black halo around you when I was in your office this morning."

A black halo around me? Strange words, strange concept. We explored it further when he later told me that he had studied with Buddhist monks and had learned to read auras.

On Tuesday, I went to my doctor and told him how I was feeling. I couldn't understand my feelings. I had an intense urge to end my life, but I had no clinical signs of depression. He asked me how I planned to do it. My immediate, matter-of-fact response was, "The same way my brother did: carbon monoxide in my garage. I can still see the marks on the inside of the overhead door from where he left his car running."

I've learned since then that it is important for doctors or others connected to a person who may be suicidal to ask them directly what their plans are. In many cases, it helps to know how serious the person is. My doctor knew I was serious because I had a plan and had articulated the plan.

People often don't share their plan, however, or they share it with someone and ask them not to tell. Two weeks before his death, my brother was with our cousin and told him that he was going to end his life. Why, oh why, did our cousin not tell us what Stuart Jr. had said? As so often happens, he likely didn't think Stuart Jr. really meant it. Would it have made a difference if he had said something? Could we have found help to get him through the crisis?

Healing Words and Letting Go

God, you know that I'm still fighting with guilt over my brother's death, over whether I could have interceded. It's too late for that now, so how do I let it go?

My child, when Stuart Jr. drove his car into the garage as you left for church that morning, you didn't know what he was going to do. You've blamed yourself so many times. It's not your fault. You've tried to figure out what you could have said or done to change the way things went that day. He wrote his goodbye note. He had already asked me to forgive him, but he also asked forgiveness of all of you in that note. He wanted you to know that he wasn't angry and didn't hold a grudge against anyone.

You read about the balance scale where it said, "Suicide is not chosen; it happens when pain exceeds resources for coping with pain." Your brother didn't have the resources to cope with the pain. He wasn't thinking clearly. He just wanted the pain to stop. He couldn't see light at the end of the tunnel. Even though I was right beside him in the car, I didn't try to stop him. I know you're struggling to make sense of that statement.

I don't want people to suffer the terrible ordeals of war. I don't want little children to be neglected, abused, or tortured. My heart breaks, as do those of the whole world, when the news screams out about children left dead in a schoolhouse from a gunman's rampage. I don't want adults to feel the devastation of their mates beating them, cheating on them, or walking out on them. I don't want my children to decide that life isn't worth living anymore.

Stuart Jr. loved me as a young child. He left me for a while as a teenager, when the rest of you did as well. But he came back again. Remember how he shared with you about his encounter with Old Charley? He and I have both met Old Charley face to face. Remember when Old Charley said that he wanted to make a deal with me at the top of the temple? Well, your brother was as strong and confident in his decision to walk away as your Lord Jesus was. He was still young, but he made the right choice. I was so proud of him.

Yes, he made mistakes and made choices he shouldn't have, but I loved him through it all. He is my child. How could I not love him? In the last few months of his life, in his time of deep pain and despair, we spent more and more time together as he talked to me about what was happening in his life.

What about you? For your whole life, you have carried the burdens of the world on your shoulders. Remember when your counselor asked why you had to be the strong one in your family? It happened after you told him about the note from your brother: "Help the family over this one." Why have you always felt it was your responsibility to carry everything for everyone? Why don't you let it go sometime and see what it feels like to let me carry the burden for you?

I saw you the night you woke up, a five-year-old child, and wandered into your parents' room. I was right beside you when you saw the blood on the sheets.

Throughout your life, I have been carrying you, just as the "Footprints" poem says. I think you like that poem because you want so desperately to believe that you're not alone, that I really am there to carry you.

I know how many times you've felt alone. I know the pain you felt all those nights when your husband didn't come home until the early morning, intoxicated and full of excuses. I know how much you hurt when he said and did the things he did.

Even when you have let me into your life to walk with you, breathing my presence deeply into your soul, you have not truly comprehended who I am and how deeply I love you.

You are a child of the King, the everlasting King, the King who knows no beginning and no end. You are not my only child, but I love to embrace you. I know everything about you. I read every thought, hear every word, feel every wound, sense every fear. I do that and, at the same time, embrace all those you love, all those who have hurt you, and all those who have caused indescribable pain for others. I love them all.

You can't comprehend it because you are not God. But I am God. I love unconditionally. I know you would like to be able to love that way, too.

How many times did you let your own wounds, your own scars, keep you from being open to the wounds of others? How many times could you have brought healing to others instead of making them feel unworthy or rejected? Do you realize that you haven't shown unconditional love to them because you haven't fully experienced it from me? It is here as a gift: my unconditional love. Take it; it's yours. In taking it, you'll be able to give it in turn to those you meet every day, wherever you walk on this earth.

You don't have to let people abuse you. You are my precious daughter. You are a child of the King and deserve the respect that position holds. Walk with your head high, smile and laugh, and let others see the words "unconditional love" written on your being. Let them experience what it means by how you live each day.

God, I can see that much of the buried hurt in my heart resulted from not truly believing that you love me unconditionally. With these insights from you, I now feel the overwhelming presence of your love. It fills me up in an indescribable way. To think that you, the God of the universe, reach down to carry me, even when I don't comprehend it, is an amazing realization. God, you are so good!

> *Every breath is an opportunity to receive and let go. I receive love and I let go of pain.*
>
> —Brenda MacIntyre[29]

---

29 Brenda MacIntyre, *FinestQuotes*, "Every breath is an opportunity…" January 14, 2014 (http://www.finestquotes.com/quote-id-28629.htm).

chapter eight
Fall from the Top

And so I wait. I wait for time to heal the pain and raise me to my feet once again—so that I can start a new path, my own path, the one that will make me whole again.

—Jessie Braun[30]

SHATTERED PLANS, SHATTERED WALL, AND SHATTERED BODY PARTS

My sister Faye and I planned to go to the Mexican Riviera one year to earn our open water scuba diving certification. My excitement grew as we booked our trip online while talking on the phone late one night. My dream for many years had been to go scuba diving in Cozumel, a world-renowned divers' paradise.

I knew this trip held all kinds of promise. After a wild ride at work for over a year, during which I took on the most challenging project of my career, I finally found a window of opportunity to get away. Things were slowing down a bit during the Christmas season.

---

30 Jessie Braun, "Starting a New Path." In *Chicken Soup for the Teenage Soul II*, ed. Jack Canfield, Mark Victor Hansen, and Kimberly Kirberger (Deerfield Beach, FL: Health Communications, 1998), 26.

Less than a month before Christmas, my dream of diving in the turquoise waters of the Caribbean ended. My life changed when I fell down thirteen steps of my house in the early morning hours. The fall happened less than an hour after Faye and I got off the phone. Besides a badly mangled and terribly painful left arm and right knee, several dents decorated the wall at the foot of the stairs.

So why the shattered plans, shattered wall, and shattered body parts?

I had dozed off after looking at my clock at 12:45 a.m. My sleep was short-lived and I woke soon afterward to the ferocious sounds of cat claws shredding the corner of my mattress. When that didn't motivate me to leap to the demands of Puddy, my five-year-old cat, he resorted to his next attention-seeking device: the most ear-piercing, turn-over-in-your-grave meowing that could possibly come out of the mouth of an otherwise adorable gray tabby cat.

That got me up in a hurry, but Puddy knew instantly that his success wasn't going to result in his desired trip outdoors. Perhaps he decided, "If I'm not getting out of the house, I might as well try to keep from getting locked downstairs." He spent the next several minutes leading me in the dark down the garden path, so to speak. After pinning Puddy at the top of the stairs, I was finally back in charge. To be on the safe side, I swooped down and picked him up by the scruff of the neck so he wouldn't use his sharp attack claws on my arms or chest.

Suddenly, I was on my way down the stairs. I recall little other than the fleeting thought that I needed to protect my head. I didn't know if I had slipped or overstepped the top stair in the dark. It seemed like I missed a few very long seconds of my life in that short time.

What could I do when people asked about what happened but blame it on the cat?

I recall lying on the floor at the bottom and staring at the indentations in the wall. They somewhat resembled those of cartoon characters who leave the outline of their bodies in walls during animated chases. At a different time, I might have been impressed to think my body had created this artwork. Unfortunately, at this moment, all I could think about was how dizzy I felt and how important it was not to pass out.

I knew I had to get to a phone upstairs to call for help. With strength that could have only come from supernatural forces, I used my uninjured bottom end, my one good arm, and opposite good leg to drag myself up the steps, moaning with pain at every movement. I finally reached the kitchen phone and called my neighbor, Rick, who answered sleepily. I told him briefly what had happened and he said he would be right over. Fortunately, he had a key to get in because he had been doing renovations at my house a few days earlier.

When Rick arrived, I broke the news to him that my battered body needed the comfort of an ambulance bed rather than a sit-up ride in his jeep. The pain was starting to settle in deeper than when I had first called him.

Broken

The next few days at the hospital were mostly a blur as I experienced the effects of morphine. I found out my left wrist was broken and my right tibia plateau, the second largest bone in the body, was crushed on the outside and fractured on the inside of my knee. I suffered severe whiplash injuries to my neck and back. Visitors were my mirror and told me that I also had several prominent scrapes and bruises on my head, knee, and other places.

The orthopedic surgeon ordered a temporary splint for my arm until the swelling subsided and they could book a day for surgery. An orthopedic brace immobilized me from hip to ankle. Before the attendant wheeled me in to the operating room for surgery on my wrist and knee three days later, the surgeon told me that I wouldn't be able to bear weight on my right leg for at least three months.

"What do you mean, no weight bearing for three months?" I said. "I'm supposed to be going scuba diving in three weeks."

Then, naïve as the question was, I asked, "Does that mean I won't be able to drive, either?" Of course, the answer was yes. I couldn't comprehend it. No walking, no driving, no scuba diving! How would I get to work, which was nearly an hour from my house?

I learned over the next few weeks what a challenge it was to use a walker, especially with an arm extension for my broken wrist. It was literally impossible to progress to using crutches at that time. One morning, a nurse came in and announced that I was going to an extended care hospital in forty-five minutes.

The ambulance came and took me to a sub-acute care bed in a nursing home. A nursing home? Yes, that's where I ended up. There was a shortage of beds in rehabilitation facilities and I found myself surrounded by seniors unable to care for themselves. At my first meal, one of the attendants came up and put a large bib around my neck. I was devastated.

I stayed there for almost two weeks. They wanted to keep me for three months, until I was able to put weight on my knee. I only escaped because I was adamant that I was checking myself out.

I assured the physiotherapist that I had an elevator at home so I wouldn't need to walk up and down my stairs. I also promised that I would have someone around to help me. Skeptical, the physiotherapist and occupational therapist took a field trip with me to my country home. They discovered I was telling the truth when I insisted that we all cram into the small elevator to ride to the second floor of the house.

Dependence, My Greatest Trial

I struggled with thoughts about my possible future over the next few months. Faye came to care for me. Losing my independence was the biggest trial of my life. I needed Faye's help for almost everything. My neighbor Rick helped, too, by driving me to the hospital and physiotherapy sessions and keeping my driveway clear of snow.

I felt total humiliation and frustration at times during the early months. I needed help getting in and out of the car when I got out of the hospital and whenever I went for appointments and errands. I struggled to navigate the house with the walker and wheelchair.

A homecare attendant had to assist me in entering and exiting the shower. I couldn't reach into the refrigerator because of my immobilizing contraptions. I couldn't stand long enough to make meals, because using the walker caused too much pain in my hips. I couldn't do laundry or housecleaning, although I did sit in my wheelchair one day and vacuum the rug, becoming totally entangled in the long vacuum hose before I finished the job.

I couldn't do simple things like open a jar lid or pill bottle or reach for water from the water cooler. I couldn't replace a DVD in the DVD player or move from one side of the bed to the other to reach my computer or phone or a book. I even needed help to pick up my socks when I dropped them on the floor. I couldn't put them on because I couldn't reach my feet, with the leg brace immobilizing me.

Then my friend, Gerrie, brought me the "grabber" daily living aid. It was a lifesaver for both Faye and me because I no longer needed her help to pick up all the things I couldn't reach. I could now grab my dresser handle and pull open the drawer and take out my own socks and other small items. Thus, my journey back to independence slowly began.

During this time of dependence on others, I gained a clearer understanding of what it means to be dependent on God. People told me throughout this experience that maybe God was trying to teach me a lesson, to get me to slow down because I was always in overdrive. My response was that God wasn't the clumsy one. I was! I fell down the stairs. He hadn't pushed me.

Let the Fun Begin

It was exciting when the orthopedic surgeon gave the go-ahead to have my arm cast and leg brace removed, and for physiotherapy to begin. He told me that my wrist was in such bad shape that it would take months of painful, aggressive therapy, and even then mobility might never come back.

I asked Melissa, my physiotherapist, to do whatever she needed to do to prove him wrong. I said I wanted to wave my hand and wrist in the doctor's face the next time I saw him in three months. I told her, "Let the fun begin."

I was thrilled to move from a range of motion of five degrees in my wrist to almost eighty degrees during that intensive physiotherapy. I took great delight in waving it at the doctor when I went for my appointment, and he was definitely impressed.

And I reached other milestones. I went from a wheelchair and walker to two crutches, then to one crutch, and finally, to a cane. I felt like a toddler taking her first steps. I also felt like an Olympic gold medal winner as I watched the Winter Olympics on TV while doing my ridiculous-looking hop-slide, throwing my arms into the air to propel myself forward. Yes, I had learned to walk again!

Then I started to drive after four months, first in my acreage subdivision as I tested out my knee flexibility and strength on the brake, then on deserted country roads. Finally, I made my first triumphant trip into my office in the city. Even more importantly, after almost six months I was able to take my German shepherd for short walks, using the cane which I finally discarded a few months later.

When I could drive again, I tried going back to work part-time and working from home part-time. But almost six months after my accident, I was diagnosed with complex regional pain syndrome (CRPS)[31] in my left hand, likely caused by the fall or surgery where one of the spikes designed to hold the bones in place got too close to a nerve. This ended my attempts to go back to work for the immediate future.

Initially, the doctor instructed me not to use my left hand at all for three months. No typing? How could I survive when the

---

31 U.S. Department of Health and Human Services, *National Institute of Neurological Disorders and Stroke*, "NINDS Complex Regional Pain Syndrome Information Page," December 23, 2013 (http://www.ninds.nih.gov/disorders/reflex_sympathetic_dystrophy/reflex_sympathetic_dystrophy.htm).

computer had become an extension of my hands at home and at work? Computer withdrawal was painful. I adapted by initiating a slow, awkward typing technique using one or two fingers of my right hand.

At the end of August that year, nine months after my fall, my doctor said I could gradually start typing for short periods with my left hand. There was no improvement. In fact, it made the pain worse, so I went back to one-handed typing. This also caused severe pain flare-ups, because the nerves are all interconnected.

In November, Melissa started me on an education program where I learned pain management techniques[32] related to CRPS. She told me to imagine one nerve sending a message to my muscles, joints, and skin, then to imagine the same nerve sending a hundred messages, instead of one. That causes chaos, confusion and pain in a person's nervous system, muscles, joints, and skin. But that's what CRPS is like.

Melissa told me this program was going to be the hardest eight to ten weeks of my life, harder than any project I had ever undertaken at work. My response was, again, "Let the fun begin!"

But it wasn't fun. For weeks, I felt like I was never going to improve. Besides physio, I had massage treatments for the whiplash injuries in my back, as well as kinesiology treatments to support me in preparing to return to work. Slowly, I started to make progress.

Under Melissa's guidance, I learned more about the medical condition of CRPS and applied breathing techniques and other methods in an attempt to reduce my pain. The swelling, coldness,

---

32 For more information, visit *Life Is Now* (http://www.lifeisnow.ca/).

numbness, stiffness, and unrelenting fire burning through my hand for months gradually began to subside. But it took almost six more months of treatments before I re-entered the workforce on a gradual return-to-work program. I had gone for almost a year unable to type anything other than minimal, one-handed, hunt-and-peck style.

I still struggle with the CRPS pain in my hand, as much from stress as from actual typing and other stressors. As Melissa said, "Stress creates cortisol, and cortisol causes pain."

Healing Words and Letting Go

God, throughout my life, I've been broken on the inside by the loss of my mother, my brother, and my marriage, as well as by fighting the battle of depression and a mood disorder. But I was gradually recovering from those life challenges.

Now, as I was looking forward to a wonderful new adventure, I ended up broken again—this time physically. Being hospitalized and needing so much care after being released left me feeling dependent, helpless, and frustrated. I also felt vulnerable about my uncertain future.

I know you allowed it for a reason, God. What lessons did you want me to learn through this experience?

My child, you had a tough time after your accident, didn't you? Here I was, giving you a wonderful example of what dependence means and all you did was resist the whole thing. No, I didn't throw you down those thirteen stairs and put you through the wall. I know that was a tough thing to go through (both the fall and the wall), but remember that "all things work together for good to them that love God" (Romans 8:28, KJV).

Tell me it hasn't been for good. Look at what happened. Your sister came almost eight hundred miles and stayed with you for all those months when you couldn't walk, and you both had an opportunity to get to know each other better than you ever had before.

You, my child, really did make some unwise choices. You had all those months when you didn't have to work, but there you were on your computer, in bed, trying to work using one hand.

I allowed you to have that gift of time, time that you could have used to get to know me better, to read my Word, to meditate, to refocus our relationship after the intense project you had been working on for almost eighteen months. You really needed that break. Seriously, it wasn't me; it was the cat! At least, that's what you told everyone. Actually, the bottom of your pajamas caught between the heel of your foot and your slipper, causing you to trip and fall in the dark.

I'm glad you've acknowledged me for helping you back up the stairs. You've said many times how much worse it could have been. You could have been knocked unconscious with no one there to find you, or paralyzed like others who had similar accidents. But you weren't. The superhuman strength you talked about was the strength I gave you to get upstairs to a telephone to call for help.

You spent several weeks recovering when you were in so much pain and didn't remember who came to visit or who phoned. Eventually, you had the opportunity to reconnect with me—and you barely did it. Here I am, your Father, the King of the universe, not a bad being to spend time with.

Sadly, you didn't even bother to give me a quick greeting in the morning most of the time, and the evenings were just as bad. Why didn't you want to spend time with me during all those months after your accident? Instead, you worked and typed, even when one arm was in a cast and in so much pain while you lay in bed, unable to walk.

Talking to me, talking with me, meditating, praying… use whatever words you want; it's all about the same thing—relationship. Our relationship! The relationship of a father and child, the relationship of a physician and patient. Most of all, it's really about two friends.

Remember the song "My God and I"? That was your song to me, when you decided you wanted a relationship with me as a young adult, when you discovered that the life you were living wasn't what you wanted anymore, when you realized that your childhood perception of me had been inaccurate.

We've had some good times, haven't we? But like any friendship, any marriage, any parent-child relationship, there are ups and downs. It doesn't have to be perfect all the time to be a relationship. Did you hear what I said? It doesn't have to be perfect to be a relationship.

In the early morning session at your retreat, you heard the words, "I am enough." Your eyes welled up with tears. You didn't believe those words about yourself, but they're true. The reason you're enough is that you're who I created you to be.

Stop being so hard on yourself. If I, the Creator of the universe, lovingly accept you as you are, who are you to deny the incredible and beautiful person I created you to be? You are enough. You are enough to be my child, my friend. You are enough to live with me in eternity. You are enough for me to use you to reach out to others who don't have the privileges you have.

I know that some of your life has been hard, but it has taught you so much that can benefit others who are still struggling. Now is your time to take all the hard lessons you have learned and make them practical parts of your life.

I know you do a lot of that. Your friend, Maria, has said more than once that you seem to have a gift for being sensitive to hurting and lonely people. It is a gift, my gift to you, the gift of mercy. Your wounded heart taught you things many people never learn. It has made it possible for you to reach out to people in ways some others can't.

It doesn't mean you are the only one with special gifts. All my children have gifts, each planned specifically for them. All babies in their mothers' wombs are born unique, which collectively makes for balance and harmony in this world. Your gift is a piece of the harmony. Unfortunately, because so many people choose not to use the gifts I give them, the world isn't harmonious. It's full of turmoil and friction, and those who need others to minister to them sometimes miss out because many of my children don't use their gifts.

So, you missed the opportunity for a better relationship between us. But I gave you a second chance, didn't I? When your diagnosis of CRPS meant you had to take more time off work, you and I had another opportunity to reconnect on a deeper level. No, I didn't cause it to happen. I could have done a miracle for you and made your medical condition disappear, but I chose not to. I knew you needed more time. I gave that time to you, hoping you were ready for our deep heart-to-heart.

You certainly find many ways to distract yourself from walking in the light. You had almost another year. How many people have that kind of gift, that time to refocus their relationship with a special friend? A whole year of not working, time to do what's most important in life, to renew the walk we started so many years ago. I give you credit for doing so many productive things with that time. That's why we're here right now. You've finally given me a chance to speak to you.

How do you like being on the other side of the conversation? You've asked me many questions, but this is the first time I've had your undivided attention in a long while. I hope it feels as good for you as it does for me. I've had so much to share with you, but you weren't ready until now.

What do you want me to share? Do you want me to talk about your circumstances? I told you earlier about some of the things that were going on so you would understand that I really was there in the midst of it all. I'm so glad you like the poem about my footprints. It speaks to your struggle with feelings of aloneness, with a sense that you had to carry the burdens of the world by yourself. I'm so sorry you have felt that way, but that tells me that you're ready to internalize the reality of who I am.

You've been so hurt in life by people who abandoned or betrayed you, but you don't comprehend on a deep level that the God of the universe isn't like that. I'm here to support you, to carry you through the rough patches of life. You may not realize this because you can't see all the footprints washed away in the sands of time—my footprints, not yours. I carried you so many times, but you didn't realize it because you didn't look back. I wish you had, just to gain a bit more appreciation of how close I've been without you even knowing it.

How I long to feel your appreciation for me. So many of my children take me for granted or don't even believe I exist. Think of the hurt you've felt when you didn't think your child appreciated you. Magnify it a billionfold and you'll hardly begin to comprehend what I yearn for. I long for every child to come back, to be safe like sheep in a sheepfold, with a shepherd keeping watch. Can you believe that I feel alone at times? Even with a heaven full of angels, I feel isolation and pain as I ache for my children to want to spend time with me.

So, thank you for giving me this time. You can ask me questions or I can just pour out my heart to you. It's up to you. You're holding the pen and can write every word I whisper in your ear, or you can censor the ones you don't want to put on the page.

Are you beginning to feel a little bit like Job yet? He challenged me with the troubles he faced. I'm always up for a challenge. Job wanted to know who I was. I gave him a picture of me, not just for his understanding, but also for the whole world to understand.

I am your Father, I am your friend, but I am also your God, King of the universe, Commander of the Heavens, Ruler of the Earth. Satan thinks he is ruler of Earth, but he isn't. He has followers on Earth, but anything he does to destroy, to desecrate, I allow. That may sound hard to comprehend, but it's all about choices. He has choices, just as you have choices. He made a choice, and that's why my Son died. My Son made a choice, and that's why you live.

You can't comprehend why so many terrible things happen in this world. Most of the world blames it on me, the one who overflows with unconditional love, acceptance, and forgiveness. I know the hearts of humankind. I created all of you. What if I had never given you a choice and you were locked into a slavery of the mind that turned you into robots?

Like Job, I expect you have a lot of questions I still haven't answered. Do you want to know about your marriage? You wanted a marriage with me at the center, but that didn't happen. You ended up knowing within a few hours after your wedding reception that it wasn't going to last, or if it was, that it was going to be hell on Earth.

I know you went into it with good intentions. I know you prayed for guidance. I know you vowed to me that you would never marry anyone who didn't believe in me. But you were only one of two people contributing to it. You can't carry the full responsibility for its failure. I saw how hard you tried. I didn't turn my back on your heart's cries for my help.

I carried you, but you didn't see my footprints. I saw the effort you put into living with love in spite of how your husband treated you. My Word clearly gives a message to the men of this world to love their wives as deeply as they love themselves. It always comes back to choices. I would never deny that. If I did, I wouldn't be God.

I saw how many nights you cried silently. I could feel the pain you held in your heart. I wanted nothing more for you than complete joy in a beautiful marriage. I feel that heart pain continually as my children around the world suffer in similar circumstances.

Oh, the wounds of the heart! You've had more than your share, but I carry the wounds of every heart that has ever beaten since time began. I want love in this world. I want others to emulate the love I have shown. I don't want people to misunderstand me, as they have for so long. Too many people point their fingers at me in response to the tragic things that happen in this world.

You know what you feel like when people misunderstand you. You feel rejected, hurt, and betrayed. Heap all of that on my Son and then see it suspended on the cross. It all comes down to the cross. All the things you and others have done to destroy self-worth and value, to betray, and to cause pain are hanging on the cross.

The word "sin" looks so small, but it is huge. SIN is almost as massive as this world itself, but FORGIVENESS is more immense than the universe. Look and see that S-I-N is buried in F-O-R-G-I-V-E-N-E-S-S. Is anything more exciting than that? More exhilarating? More inspiring? When you went to the Grand Canyon, you stood in awe. It was almost three hundred miles long, up to eighteen miles across and a mile deep. Call it "forgiveness," then take sin and throw it in. Sin is only a speck, a tiny pebble in comparison.

God, how can any of us comprehend you and your love? Your acceptance and forgiveness? What do I do with what I learn about you? Do I need to understand it? Do I need to do anything with it? Analyze it? Take it apart and dissect it? Put it back together and look at it again?

I don't know how a finite being can even scratch the surface of what you are and what you want for us. Oh God, just writing the words "what you want for us" fills me with something I cannot even describe.

I am a mother. I did the best I could with no imprinting, no modeling from a mother to show me what love and acceptance mean. I always did the best I could. I will no longer belittle myself for my shortcomings. I expect I could have done better if I had been in complete alignment with you at all times, but I wasn't.

I am letting go of my regrets because regrets eat you up, beat you up, and make you feel worthless. God, I know that's not what you want for me. You want me to know that you love me, just the way I am. Your love and acceptance will change me into the beautiful vision you have for my life. Just as I want only the best for my daughter, you want the best for me.

> *Letting go means accepting things that cannot be. It means maturing and moving on, no matter how hard you have to fight yourself to do so.*
>
> —Unknown

part five

Learning to Let Go

Before we can hope to make a real new beginning in life, we must deliberately release our old claims upon it; for it is only in letting go of whatever binds us to our past that we are free to realize the promise of who we may yet be.

—Guy Finley[33]

---

33 Guy Finley. *Life of Learning Foundation*: www.guyfinley.org. Excerpt from "The Secret of Letting Go" (http://www.guyfinley.org/free-content/video/4220). Used with permission.

chapter nine
Making Choices

Any change, any loss, does not make us victims… no matter what your situation, you can always do something. You always have a choice and the choice can be power.

—Blaine Lee [34]

CONFIDENCE AND JOY

The Choices Seminar, led by Thelma Box, was the most powerful experience in my adult life, and it stepped up my path to healing. The mission of the program is "changing the world one heart at a time."

This five-day live-in intensive program helped me to see who I was, why I was, and what I needed to do to become the person I longed to be. Over sixty people from all walks of life and areas of the country came together to open themselves to scrutiny and allow Thelma, her team of assistants, and other participants to challenge them.

---

34 Blaine Lee, *Goodreads*, "Blaine Lee Quotes," December 24, 2013 (http://www.goodreads.com/author/quotes/379706.Blaine_Lee).

I decided to go to Choices because a young woman from my church, a former schoolmate of my daughter's, had attended several months before and came back a changed person. Becky told me briefly about the program. I was really interested, so she shared a brochure with more details. She seemed to know what she wanted in life. She exuded confidence and a calm and peaceful spirit.

Why had I not seen myself the same way? I realized that all my adult life I had been fighting a lack of confidence, but I compensated by appearing overly confident and unintentionally misleading others. Becky seemed to have discovered what I lacked. Like Dorothy and her friends in the Land of Oz, on their way to obtain what they each felt was missing in their lives, I knew I needed to go to Choices to get a dose of confidence.

Several other people I knew revealed that they had attended the program and come back happier than they had ever been. I wanted more joy in my life. For most of my life, others have seen me as a very serious person. Often in formal meetings and small group discussions, people would ask why I was frowning even when I thought I was smiling. Joy was on my agenda for change.

I finally scheduled time off work and went, armed with false confidence and expectancy of a new life. I don't recall much of what took place that first afternoon and evening. I saw large banners around the room, prominently displayed. One said, "I cannot heal or change what I do not acknowledge." I wondered if I was ready to acknowledge my pain in that room full of so many strangers. Thelma led large-group interactions and the teaching assistants (TAs) led the small groups.

What stood out most about the evening session is that each person in the small group shared something traumatic about their lives. Partway through, one of the women in my group became very emotional and left. Before the evening was over, another woman excused herself, so we ended up with a very small group. I recall speaking of my mother's death, expressionless, emotionless, and I couldn't understand why others got upset so easily.

Stick Person

The next morning was the most significant in moving me forward. Thelma had drawn a visual image of a stick person on chart paper and started talking about the wounds of the heart. She used such simplistic examples that at first I became annoyed. What did she know of wounds of the heart?

What had I come here for? To hear of people's insignificant problems—that someone's parent got upset and said something unkind one day which affected the individual for a lifetime? Some of us had faced much bigger issues. But as Thelma kept talking and marking up the stick person, I felt the pain set in.

I started to sob, heaving sobs. I couldn't hold them back, even though I tried. Thelma had said to "play hard." This wasn't playing. Thelma stopped talking and her solemn demeanor changed. She had been tough on some of the participants the day before, but she kindly and gently asked me why I was crying. I told her, waving my hand at her drawing, "This is nothing. You talk about wounds of the heart. These aren't wounds of the heart. I've had *real* wounds of the heart."

Then the words poured out. With everyone in the room listening, I told Thelma about the wounds of my childhood when my mother died, the wounds of my young adult life when my brother died, my abusive marriage and divorce, and some other major life challenges I had faced. I don't remember the rest of the interchange or follow-up comments. I do know that this was a life-defining few minutes, because I became vulnerable and acknowledged my pain, something so out of character for me.

The Bean Game

That afternoon, Thelma took the participants through an exercise called the "bean game." Everyone received a small handful of beans. We took turns going around the circle and looking into each other's eyes. We told other participants if we had medicine for them and shared the beans with those we thought needed medicine most. Surprisingly, several people gave me beans. I ended up with more than almost anyone else in the room.

The lesson I internalized that day was the importance of letting others know when I am hurting and need support. They are usually more than willing to open their hearts to offer medicine and healing. This was a major shift from my usual approach of keeping things inside and not sharing my feelings with others.

Prickly Porcupine

I really disliked one of the TAs. Bob came across as arrogant, and I wondered why they would have someone like him in the room to help people go through a healing process. The TAs gave all of us new names and I seethed inside as Bob pinned a nametag with the words "Prickly Porcupine" on my sweater. He shouted, so everyone around could hear, that I kept my quills sticking out to keep other people from getting close to me.

My resentment toward him continued to build. The hardest part about what he said was that it was true. That's what I had done most of my adult life: I kept people away with my prickly quills. Now I was learning new behaviors, reprogramming myself so people would treat me differently. "We teach people how to treat us," stated another banner on the wall. Those words helped me focus on that concept.

One highlight of those five days was when Thelma put us into small teams and gave us a project. She told us that we had to learn a song and perform it the next day. I am very self-conscious about singing in front of family members, let alone sixty people whom I don't know, so I was rather reticent. Three other women and I were told we had to perform the Tina Turner version of "Proud Mary." We walked away with the lyrics on paper to search for the music track, and then we went to a second-hand store to buy fitting attire for the performance.

The following day, I became a changed person. Previously, I would have never walked into a room wearing an outfit like the one I had put on, not even at Halloween. On this day, I would have made Tina Turner proud with my choice of clothing, hairdo, and makeup. Nobody even recognized me when I stood three feet away from the group, waving to catch their attention.

I still find it hard to believe what happened when it was our turn to perform. I literally came alive and exploded in front of the crowd. I sang even though I don't sing ordinarily. I danced even though I don't dance. I flew even though I don't fly. It's amazing what happens when we don't hold back and just let go. How freeing that performance was!

Guess who smiled the broadest and cheered the loudest? Bob, Mr. Prickly Porcupine man! He even had to slow me down when the song came to an end, because I kept racing around the room, singing at the top of my lungs. He was concerned I might crash through the crowd with the momentum I had gained. Did he ever change over the course of a few days!

Or did I?

My Contract

One significant aspect of the program was a process where we made a contract—in essence, a commitment to ourselves. We expressed the words in the present tense as a way of defining who we wanted to be. When I went through that process, the words that unfolded were "I am a wonderful and joyful woman."

I had gone to Choices with the intent of returning home confident and joyful. As I thought about my contract over the next few weeks, I decided that the word "wonderful" didn't resonate as clearly as "confident" did, and I still wanted to commit to confidence. I now had another tool in my toolkit, another motto on the wall: "Be, do, have. Be committed to do what it takes to have what you want." I applied what I had learned and solved the issue by dropping "wonderful" and adding "confident" to the words of my contract—and that is what I became: someone with confidence and joy.

Over the next six months, I went through a few similar but shorter weekend sessions that were part of the Choices program. I expanded the words of my contract into a purpose statement: "I am a joyful, confident, and trusting woman of God, touching people's lives with love."

More recently, as a result of my work with people challenged with depressive illness, I revised the statement further to read: "I am a joyful, confident, and trusting woman of God, touching people's lives with love and shining a light to bring hope in the darkness."

Making the choice to acknowledge my pain and let it go brought me to a deeper level of healing, and a greater sense of purpose, than I had ever experienced before.

Healing Words and Letting Go

God, I am so thankful that the Choices program came into my life. It has made such a difference in how I deal with challenges, and with my responses to the choices other people make. Most importantly, it gave me a greater appreciation for my purpose in life, so I am thankful for that.

—⁂—

My child, yes, I gave you an amazing purpose statement. "I am a joyful, confident, and trusting woman of God, touching people's lives with love." Remember how excited you were as you absorbed what it meant to be a woman of God who touches people's lives with love? When people asked you what your purpose statement was, you shared those words with deep awe. You said that touching people's lives with love was the most incredible gift you had ever received, because those words embodied who I am.

You asked, "What could be better than that?" The answer: nothing could be better than that. You have the gift of unconditional love through Jesus' life and death. That gift is your heritage, a way to live your life every moment and every day. It doesn't have to be hard. It can be as simple as the things your friend Gerrie does, like sending daily emails of encouragement when your cat went missing. Children of mine, you really don't get it sometimes. You're so busy with yourselves that you don't take care of your sisters and brothers. You're all looking so hard for acceptance and love that you forget that you're here to be acceptance and love.

My child, you don't have to walk in the shadows of doubt and sadness, of frustration and pain, of turmoil and anxiety. I made you in my image. You can step into the light of the presence of your Savior, the one who said he would never leave you or forsake you.

Let me show you a beautiful world. Yes, it is a beautiful world in spite of all the pain, because it is my creation immersed in my love.

Touching people's lives with love... God, I imagine that's a purpose you have for all your children. You tell us that you made mankind in your image, an image of love. What would this world be like if we all lived fully in love? We can choose to do that if we choose to let you live inside us. What a powerful opportunity we have to change the world, within our immediate sphere of influence or on a global scale, by touching people's lives with love.

> *I'm a little pencil in the hand of a writing God, who is sending a love letter to the world.*
>
> —Mother Teresa[35]

---

35 Mother Teresa, *Goodreads*, "Mother Teresa Quotes," December 24, 2013 (http://www.goodreads.com/author/quotes/838305.Mother_Teresa).

chapter ten
Going with the Flow

Feelings are much like waves, we can't stop them from coming but we can choose which one to surf.
—Jonatan Mårtennson[36]

I Want to Be Free

I have struggled to let go and release the physical pain within my body through myofascial release techniques,[37] which involve gentle, sustained pressure into one's connective tissue. This type of treatment releases restrictions, reduces pain, improves motion throughout the body, and even reduces trauma from the past.

I have also struggled to let go of the pain caused by heart wounds. The hardest part in both cases has been coming into an awareness of things I didn't know, such as not knowing that I was holding onto so much physical pain, which I discovered at the myofascial release physiotherapy sessions. When I was there, I actually

---

36 Jonathan Mårtensson, *QuotesInternet*, "Emotions Quote," July 28, 2014 (http://www.quotesinternet.com/quote/13351.html)

37 For more information, visit http://myofascialrelease.com/.

learned to let out the pain as I moaned, groaned, and even screamed at one point. I know I only partially released what I had been holding onto, still afraid of what those in the next room might think. For most of my life, I've been afraid of what others might think.

I want to be free. I want to fly high, unencumbered in a hot air balloon at sunrise. I want to be untethered, not held back by a safety rope like the one that connected me to a parasailing boat a few years ago. What better metaphor could there be for letting go than a hot air balloon ride?

I need to work more on releasing pain through myofascial treatments. In the same way, I need to work on letting go of the pain of the past through whatever means will bring healing.

It took so many years for me to discover that I had pain. One night, when I was talking with Sandy, a homeschooling friend, I told her about some of my experiences. She asked me, "How do you get rid of your anger?"

"What anger?" I asked.

"You must be full of anger because of all that has happened to you."

Anger was a foreign word to me—it didn't make sense. "What do you mean, get rid of my anger?"

"When I'm angry, I punch pillows," Sandy said. "Some people smash things. Some people swear. Don't you ever do anything like that?"

Puzzled, I replied, "No. Why would a person act that way?"

"It's a form of release, a way of letting go. It's not good to keep it all bottled up inside."

Over the years, I've read books, taken courses, attended retreats, and prayed, hoping to understand what it means to let go.

White Water

I've often heard the phrase "go with the flow." Sadly, it reminds me of a good friend's son who died in a whitewater kayaking accident. He and another friend were in dangerous rapids on raging springtime waters in the mountains. His friend got into trouble and Mark tried to rescue him. The friend lived, but Mark disappeared and was never found. The family had a memorial service for him on the banks of the river in his hometown. At the service, someone spoke the words, "Gone with the flow." What a tragic way to go with the flow.

I see going with the flow as letting go of what's holding me back, allowing the waters to carry me. When I went on a whitewater rafting adventure, the river carried me. We went with the flow, our bodies moving and turning as part of the journey.

It made me think of life as a river with twists and turns, with tree branches and other items damming up sections of it. I sometimes wonder how people have the courage to let go of the riverbank, allowing the river to carry them downstream, often to places they don't know exist, and still maneuver enormous obstacles so successfully.

Prison of Fear

My sister Faye understands what it means to let go and go with the flow. She has been an expert downhill and cross-country skier, racing down the mountainside at breakneck speeds. She has kayaked on whitewater rapids and on the sea. Name the adventure—canoeing down rivers on extended trips, swimming, scuba diving, sailing on the ocean—she has seized every experience in front of her and then looked for more.

I've learned over the years that my prison of fear held me back in so many ways. One summer, Faye wanted to teach my young daughter and me how to sea kayak. She wanted to take us to Salt Spring Island on the West Coast, apparently a beautiful place to kayak. I didn't want to go, thinking that there were too many issues to consider. My daughter was too young. We had never kayaked before. We needed to practice somewhere first. We weren't equipped for an overnight camping trip. I had already made other plans.

So we parted, with negative feelings between us. All Faye wanted to do was share her passion. All I wanted was to keep my daughter and myself safe and to do the things we had already planned. I've let many opportunities go by the wayside because of fear—which I know now is a form of resistance—of not letting go.

When I finally came to understand what it meant to let go at the Choices program, when I released some of my pain and made myself vulnerable to others, it was incredibly freeing. I emerged from my cocoon and became a butterfly. I felt more vibrant than ever before. The exhilaration of those few minutes as I danced and sang didn't disappear once the performance was over.

Instead, I carried that experience for months. I was on a perpetual high. My daughter thought I was high on drugs. An old business associate saw me two months later and asked if I was in love. I said yes; I was in love with myself, the first time in my life when I was in love with me. Before that, the prison that held me was built from the scar tissue left behind by heart wounds. I received a beautiful gift of freedom when I let go.

Each experience that takes me out of my comfort zone is part of the process of letting go and going with the flow. Now I like doing things I'm afraid of just to face my fears—taking on new challenges in my career, in relationships, and in physical adventures.

My doctor told me a few years after my bipolar disorder diagnosis that I'm more fortunate than most: I have the privilege of feeling life in ways that many others can't feel. He wished that he could be like that, because the fluctuating highs and lows in my life make for a more fascinating existence than being on an even keel from day to day.

Being on an even keel… that brings up new images now, since I've gained from Faye a little understanding of sailing. The keel of a sailboat, depending on the direction and the winds, can be centered or heeled over. Faye loves the excitement of the boat being heeled over. She's given me a little taste of that by introducing me to different outdoor sports.

Stuck on a Rock

The year after I went to Choices and got over many of my fears, Faye and I went on a sea-kayaking trip. After having taken a few day trips the previous year, for practice, we decided to go on a five-day trip to Desolation Sound on the West Coast. After arriving at our departure point, we packed our gear into kayaks and started paddling up the coast.

It was a beautiful day in a scenic environment. As we came to the Point, a place where currents from several directions come together, the winds picked up and we decided to make a direct line for the opposite shore, hoping to avoid the intersection of waves from the cross currents. We pointed our kayaks and paddled. It was close to a mile to the nearest island. The first few hundred feet weren't too difficult, even though the cross currents challenged us. Then the wind came up and I felt the waves splash higher and higher over my kayak. The currents pushed strongly against us as we paddled on.

Physical strength and endurance weren't among my greatest assets, but Faye was strong, an athlete capable of scrambling up mountains. Even fit men couldn't keep up with her. When I visited her each year, she'd run for one or two hours in the early morning, then come into the house as I crawled out of bed and say, "Let's get going. I need some exercise." We would go on daylong activities that exhausted me while energizing her.

As we continued on to the island that afternoon, I kept struggling and she kept checking on me as I paddled. I complained and she encouraged. She finally slowed down, came alongside me, and tied my boat to hers. Then she—with the strength of two people— and I—struggling to keep going—continued on, fighting the wind and waves. After a while, we reached a small island which hadn't been our planned destination.

Faye was ready to explore the other nearby islands, but all I could think about was being tired and afraid. I told her I didn't think I was strong enough to paddle anymore in that weather, so we remained in our tent for most of the next few days, keeping out of the storm and waiting for the wind, waves, and rain to subside. But we bonded. We talked about things we had never talked about before. We shared our feelings about our mother's and Stuart Jr.'s deaths.

Faye told me that the only person in our family who had really taken an interest in her was Stuart Jr. If he had been alive, he would have watched her compete in the Canadian Women's National Whitewater Kayaking competition and cheered her on to second place. No one from the family had seen her triumph or joined her in celebration.

She and I hadn't been in touch much after university. That was when she got involved in whitewater kayaking and other adventurous outdoor activities and began moving from place to place. I had no idea what she was doing. I knew nothing about kayaking. I knew nothing about the significance of competing in the national whitewater kayaking competition and winning second place.

I was hurting for both of us when she spoke about the loss of someone who had cared about those important aspects of her life. I felt that I had cheated myself by not getting to know my older sister. It was a good time for both of us, for healing some of the past hurts.

Paddling Home

Finally, Faye and I decided it was time to head back to the mainland. We had left a telephone message for one of her friends, telling her to contact the Coast Guard if we didn't get back by a certain date. That day was almost upon us, so we packed up and started out early in the morning with rain falling lightly, the wind and waves having decreased. I preferred to paddle close to the shoreline, then cross to the mainland where the cross currents weren't so strong. We knew it would be a longer trip, but we would also be better protected from the elements.

When we left the rock that had been our home for the previous few days, the wind and rain started to pick up again. It was easier paddling than the day we had arrived. Unfortunately, we hadn't realized that we would have to paddle at least twice as far by going this way. Maybe the shorter route wouldn't have been so hard, after all, since we had started out so early and were rested and strong.

But we kept going on the longer route, almost twenty-five miles. When we neared the shore of the mainland, we hugged it as tightly as the waves would let us. Faye pointed out beautiful coral and barnacles where the water was lower. She always took such delight in everything she saw, in the uniqueness of each leaf, starfish, and any other treasures of nature.

Fatigue soon set in and the cold from the increasing rain and splashing waves seemed to penetrate right through our gear. We stopped a few times to take a break and realized that hypothermia was a real possibility. At one point, Faye was shaking so badly that I thought she might collapse. We finally crossed from the rocky mainland to a nearby island, because it was getting late and we needed to camp for the night. We had been paddling for over twelve hours, and we knew we couldn't paddle the remaining ninety minutes to reach our car on the mainland before dark.

As we dragged our kayaks and ourselves onto the bank, I burst into hysterical laughter and couldn't stop. Faye knew I was hypothermic, so she helped me take off my outer clothing and wrap myself in something warm, which was a real challenge with the rain still coming down.

The next day, we left the island. The skies were sunny and the waters calm. What a wonderful ending to our trip. We playfully surfed the huge but gently rolling waves. Faye told me that it was often like that when she went whitewater kayaking. She would surf the waves and go with the flow.

Healing Words and Letting Go

God, as I reflect back on my trip with my sister, I think about how much healing came to us. Why did that close relationship not remain? Why have we continued to struggle in our relationship over time?

My child, *a few days of talking doesn't take away all the pain. Relationships are about ups and downs. They are dynamic and change like ocean waves. Just as you learned the importance of going with the flow when the waves carried you toward the shore, you need to go with the flow in life and let go of your relationship wounds of the past.*

You're both learning that now. You came from the same childhood circumstances, but saw those events from different perspectives. That has affected you all of your lives. Peeling off the layers to find healing has been difficult.

You have both dealt with difficult health issues in recent years which affected your hopes and dreams for the future. Look at the world through your sister's eyes and think of what she has lost—it's so much more than you have. Then look at how she has turned her trials into a life of gratitude.

"Rejoice in the Lord always" (Philippians 4:4). Rejoicing means being grateful, which fills your heart to overflowing. When you look at everything through that lens, it pushes out the negativity, anger, sadness, despair, and pain. It gives you a new focus in life, a focus on the abundance you have because of the gifts I keep giving you. Healing from the past is a beautiful and natural consequence of gratitude.

God, rejoicing is really the same as being grateful. If I want to live a life of joy—of rejoicing—then all I need to do is make gratitude the focus of my life. That can have a major impact on the type of relationships we have with you and with family and friends. No wonder you tell us to "rejoice in the Lord always"! A continual state of gratitude changes both our thinking and behavior as we open our minds to your goodness.

> *I choose to live with a grateful heart, eyes wide open to your goodness.*
>
> —Kay Warren[38]

---

38 Kay Warren, *Choose Joy Because Happiness Isn't Enough* (Grand Rapids, MI: Revell, 2012), 254.

chapter eleven
Trusting God

God can heal a broken heart, but he has to have all the pieces.
—Author Unknown

TRUSTING BRINGS HEALING

*G*od, remind me again that healing comes from you, that triumph over pain comes from you, that renewing our focus and purpose in life comes from you.

My child, I love you with an unending love. I have loved you from eternity. I have loved you from the moment you were conceived. I have loved you through everything that has happened in your life. I will never leave you or abandon you. I want you to be happy. Even more than that, I want you to trust me. I shaped the words of the contract you made for yourself, that you are a "trusting woman of God."

Do you trust me? Do you really trust me? Do you trust me enough to let go of the wounds of your heart? To let go of the pain inside that caused you to build walls that are tough to penetrate? The scar tissue is hard to break down, because those scars have accumulated for over fifty years, layer upon layer building on top on each other, never released.

I know you didn't want that to happen. You wanted to remain that beautiful blonde-haired child who, in spite of losing your mother, continued to be bubbly, talkative, and joyful. But circumstances change people, and they have changed you.

You learned the art of survival. You didn't shed the tears you should have shed when you were young. As you release the pain, every moan, every groan, every cry is a story of the hurt and tears held inside that you didn't release sooner. I'm not blaming you. You were a child with no one to teach you. I saw you work hard over the years to make sense of how to deal with both the open wounds and the scars.

Sometimes you have given me permission to take away your pain. It's a process. You can't just pray for release and see it happen instantly every time. Yes, I have performed miracles. I could have performed one for you, but I knew you needed a different approach. You needed to learn over time to experience both joy and pain, because together they have taught lessons that are important for you to learn.

My ways are not your ways. I choose when I want to use one approach or when I choose a different one for my children. I know you want to get in the middle of the healing process and take away from me the gift I want to give you, when I know you're ready. You just need to let go and trust the process.

I didn't heal everyone physically when I was on the earth, but I did choose a small number of people to heal immediately. Everywhere I went, people were clawing at my clothes, including the woman who hung desperately onto the bottom of my coat until I healed her. People begged me to come to their homes—the centurion whose daughter had died, and Mary and Martha, whose brother Lazarus had died. I left Lazarus to decay for four days so people would understand what death is.

Have you ever stopped to think about the diversity of healing approaches I've used? Have I always applied the same methods? No, because those people were individuals, each as unique as everything else I have created. There is beauty in what I have created, and beauty in what I healed and recreated.

Do you think I didn't heal others just because you haven't read their stories? So many people listened to me, touched me, and saw me on the cross. Many had to do heart work, too. Some had such deep wounds of the heart that they believed they would never recover.

Some people thought I didn't care about them when I didn't reach out and heal them right away. How could I not heal everyone I met? I chose not to heal their physical problems because I knew some of my children needed heart healing even more than physical healing.

Someday you will meet those I have healed, and they will tell you their stories. Some will tell of waking up one day after I left the earth and discovering that the pain in their leg, or their leprosy, or internal health problems had vanished. It's kind of like a birthday present. For some of them, the timing wasn't right for healing when I was there, but when it was right they got the gift they wanted so desperately.

You will meet others who say that they, too, were disappointed, that it seemed like I didn't listen to their pleas. I knew all of them intimately. I knew that the greater gift would be the therapy that gradually releases scar tissue from the heart. Many people will have amazing stories of how I healed them on a deeper level when I walked the earth.

Spiritual healing, the healing that takes place when you think you aren't worthy, when you long for acceptance and then realize you have it—oh, that is the greatest gift! All through the ages, people have *struggled so much, feeling that they had no right to walk with me, that what they did was impossible to forgive. I know you're one of them. You have thought many times that you didn't deserve my grace. You didn't believe I could forgive you. But* "it is by grace you have been saved, through faith—and this is not from yourselves, it is the gift of God" *(Ephesians 2:8).*

You children of mine are alike in so many ways as you struggle to make sense of life. I had a sense of humor when I created you and planted such complex feelings and emotions inside you. Oh, I love you all with an everlasting love! You don't weary me with all your questions and doubts. You just don't comprehend who I am, or how deep and wide my love is.

I spoke about the Grand Canyon earlier. I was talking about sin, about throwing it in and letting it fall, that it is only a grain of sand in the canyon of my love. I embrace you from the moment you wake up in the morning until you fall asleep at night, and all through the night I send my warmth and love to you and through you. Why don't you feel my love? Why don't you understand my love? Why don't you believe my love?

I want so badly to be in constant communion with you, to open your eyes to who I really am. All you need to do is allow yourself to let go—of past disappointments, of hurts, of the baggage you continue to drag with you. You can bring it all to me. When you come and spend a few minutes in my presence, you will understand more, see more, feel more, and love more.

By beholding, you become changed. Behold me in the morning, in the evening, at noon. Behold me in the beauty of the world I created for you. Behold me in everyone who says a kind word or gives you a smile, everyone who embraces you and accepts you as you are.

Yes, my child, let the words of the song "Just as I Am" keep playing through your head. I love to hear you sing it to me, and I sing it to you, too. Just as I am, I come to you to love you, to walk with you through the valley and on the mountaintop, and if you need it, to pick you up and carry you across the sand.

I know the end from the beginning. I know all about you. I know about your mother and all the sadness she experienced. I know that you believe depression is a sign of weakness. You're getting past those feelings to some extent, but it doesn't take much to bring them back when someone makes a comment to you at church about how people wouldn't be depressed if they just trusted God. You and many others think depression is a lack of trust in me.

Think about it. Not one of my children has been in spirit with me every moment of every day. Those who make comments—about you not trusting me when you're dealing with mental health issues—have such a limited understanding of who I am. I long for them to comprehend me. How deeply it hurts to see my children in pain.

You've spent a lot of time wandering in the wilderness, sometimes doubting, sometimes trusting. At times, you were open to receive me just as a child is open, but sometimes you have wanted to make sense of your world on your own. You didn't trust where I wanted to take you and why. You didn't need to know all the answers. You just needed to look at me.

To be free of those heart wounds, you needed to let go and figuratively picture yourself sailing into the sky, just as you want to do in that hot air balloon you are planning to ride in some day. You needed to trust me more, and you needed to absorb so many more lessons. You have received them now as a gift from me, because you have opened your heart to my deep love.

God, I see the footprints in the sand. I see the times when I bled openly and didn't let go. Yes, if only I had trusted more. If only I had let go and let you come in and wipe away my tears and heal my hurts. If only I had allowed myself to walk the daily path with you when you wanted to take me places where I was resistant to go. What a difference that would have made in my life.

I'm ready to start here and now, looking forward to walking more closely with you in the future.

> *The beautiful journey of today can only begin when we learn to let go of yesterday.*
>
> —Steve Maraboli[39]

---

[39] Dr. Steve Maraboli, *Unapologetically You: Reflections on Life and the Human Experience* (Port Washington, NY: A Better Today Publishing, 2013), 29.

chapter twelve
Breaking Down Heart Walls

The walls we build around us to keep sadness out also keep out the joy.

—Jim Rohn[40]

THE IMPRINT OF LOVE

When I first came to comprehend that God knew me before I was born, it was more than I could absorb, leaving me overwhelmed. My mother hadn't wanted me. She had wanted my aunt and uncle to adopt me before I was even born. But who had wanted me? My God, my Father! In my mother's womb, he imprinted a story on me that is more powerful than the message my mother wrote on my tiny unborn heart.

I am deeply sorry for my mother's pain, her struggles, all she went through that brought her to the place where she felt incapable of caring for and nurturing the seed growing inside her. I know her life was hard. I try to rationalize it, and sometimes I do

---

40 Jim Rohn, *Facebook*, "The walls we build ..." March 13, 2013 (https://www.facebook.com/OfficialJimRohn/posts/10152620803745635).

it effectively. How I wish she had known that the seed of hope, love, and acceptance from God was inside her own mother's womb before she was born.

Why did I discover it and she didn't? Did she know God and still succumb to the darkness brought on by her illness? What if I had taken my own life in a time of deep despair? Would people have said that I hadn't believed in God? Would they have understood the pain that comes from depression? For those who haven't experienced it, how could they know? I didn't know until I lived and breathed it myself.

HEALING WORDS AND LETTING GO

When you wall others out, you also wall yourself in.
—Joyce Meyer[41]

Heart walls! God, thank you for helping me understand that to live with joy, I need to let the heart walls come down. They are so thick that it could take years of chipping away to break them down. Or, in an instant, they could come down if you took a huge mallet and struck hard.

My child, be patient. An instant blow to the walls of the heart could result in extreme pain. I could do it, but it would be even more difficult than chipping away at them. I am willing to break down the walls, if you let me,

---

[41] Joyce Meyer, *Twitter*, "When you wall others out..." February 15, 2013 (https://twitter.com/Joyce-Meyer/status/302550912189218818).

Chapter Twelve: Breaking down Heart Walls • 157

but it cannot be in your time. I can't have you rush me or slow me down. I know what I'm doing. I can see where the walls come up close against blood vessels and heart muscle. This is an intricate process. This is heart surgery in its purest form.

I have wanted to perform this operation on you for so long. I have seen the accumulation and thickening of the walls. With each wound of the heart, I've seen another layer add to the thickness and depth—cold granite layering atop the soft tissue pressed against your heart. It's dangerous to allow growths like that to take over the heart. Although I've wanted to help you, I would never impose myself upon you if you didn't choose to let me.

> *I will give you a new heart and put a new spirit in you; I will remove from you your heart of stone and give you a heart of flesh.*
>
> —Ezekiel 36:26

God, to live my purpose in life, to touch people's lives with love, I need you to do your work. I need you to take over and do what is necessary to give me a healthy heart, a heart that is open and willing to receive love so I can, in turn, give love. I need to be able to accept whatever comes to me with that open heart and take the things that hurt me and turn them into something good. How can a person protect themselves from pain if their heart is wide open, exposed to everything the world has to give, good or bad?

My child, if you aren't open, wide open, you'll never be able to take in all the love I have for you. You will never feel the amazing goodness I offer you. You will never feel the full acceptance of my grace for you. How can you fathom any of this if you only let a hairline crack of my love seep into you?

You are missing so much. The goodness and love that want to come in are so much better than the things you are blocking out. I am greater than the universe and you deny me full entrance into your heart because you're trying to keep out the things that hurt. Don't you think I can immerse you so fully in my love that everything else will pale in significance to what I offer?

You've missed so many opportunities to let my joy fill you up. When you were younger, you were more open than you have been for most of your adult life. It's time to let go again, to release the fear and let me have my way with your heart walls. I want only the best for you. You don't have to be afraid. Let me do the surgery and open your heart fully. I know you want to live the rest of your life with purpose and joy and love. Trust me. I will keep waiting for a day, a week, a year. I will even wait until eternity if I have to. The longer you put it off, the longer you will live with regret, because you'll look back at the years you could have lived differently.

Oh, my child, my heart is so full and I want yours to be full as well. You have sung many songs about my spirit and love filling you up, but somehow you have missed the importance of letting me do the work to make that possible. Will you let me open the walls? It will help to heal the wounds of your heart. You have no idea what's in store for you. Trust me, my child.

God, as I look back, I wonder how many times I have kept out joy and love to protect myself from pain and hurt. What about the relationships in my life? With my daughter? With family members? With friends? It's sad to think that the effect of our choices has a snowballing effect on other aspects of our lives. God, what are you trying to teach me through this? I know I could have had a richer, fuller, joy-filled life if I hadn't allowed the walls to block out the goodness of life. Would I be able to love more fully? I believe I would.

I want to live a life of joy, filled with your spirit. Besides blocking out opportunities for joy and love, have I inadvertently blocked out the joy I could have had with you all these years? Are the heart walls just a way of keeping you out when you want so badly to come into my life?

As a child, I sang a song called "Into My Heart," about you coming into my heart and shining out. I sang it so many times. As an adult, I sang it again when I led children's programs at church. Did I have any comprehension of what it meant? Intellectually—in my head, in my mind, in my thinking—I believed I understood, but I didn't internalize it. I didn't realize that it was impossible for you to come in when my heart walls block you.

My marriage took a huge toll on my relationship with you. There was pain, so much pain. My marriage is when I began to lay down all those layers of heart protection. It started with the first time my husband pierced my heart with his words. It continued through the years. Every time he plunged in the knife, it caused me to protect myself more.

I blocked out so many feelings. I was no longer capable of letting in love. I chose to let the walls protect me. I did it for my own survival, but in allowing that to happen, I denied myself a rich and fulfilling life. I became incapable of loving others deeply. I could speak of love and show a degree of love for others, but the profound experience of love has not been a part of me.

If I had really allowed love to flow in and out, just as people breathe in and out, would it have made a difference in my relationships with others? I have some deep heart work to do. I realize now that I have no true comprehension of the meaning of love, of God's love, of love from people. Where do I go now, God?

My child, what if my Son had put up heart walls? What if the wounds of his heart caused him to protect himself, as you have been doing? Where would he be now? Where would you be? Where would all my other children be?

Jesus was wounded for what my children have done. Do you understand what that means? He had such deep wounds of the heart that it is incomprehensible. I, his Father, did not live in human form as he did. But as I watched from heaven, every knife that pierced his heart pierced my heart, too.

We are one. Every word spoken, every physical act against him, filled me with pain so intense that you would never be able to experience it if you went down to the bottom of the deepest ocean or climbed the highest mountain. You would not feel it or understand it if you took a spaceship into the furthest reaches of the universe. My love, and the love of my Son, is so unimaginable, so unfathomable, that it will take immeasurable time when we're together for you to grasp even a little bit of what it really means.

When you read about the closing hours of Jesus' life on Earth as he hung on the cross, you think that you understand what it meant. That poem I gave you as a young adult, "Go Tell the World," spoke of our love, but it hardly touched the surface of what that love is like. Besides the agony Jesus went through on the cross, and I in the darkness beside him, his whole life on Earth was filled with hurt and pain.

He never denied it. He never blocked it out. He never put up walls to his heart. If he had, he wouldn't have been able to come into my presence daily, hourly, moment by moment so we could commune together and plan how he could walk each day and survive those hurts. His heart was open to me, his Father. If he had closed it off, he and I would have lost the opportunity to connect and keep our wonderful relationship healthy and vibrant.

You're finally beginning to grasp it. If you're willing, you can be completely open to whatever goodness and light I bring to you. I know your heart is opening a little bit now. I see the tears in your eyes. I hear the deep breathing and feel with you the weight of emotion on your chest. You're still a child, coming before me, mature in years, but young in your desire to explore and understand, with a craving for something better than you have. Everything is waiting for you, my child—a better life that will bring you into a closer walk with me in spite of your circumstances.

You've had deep pain, and you never fully experienced the goodness of God because of it. How I wish you had learned those lessons sooner. I know you do, too, because you've missed so much in life. But we're together now and can begin the journey anew. Look at it as starting fresh—being born again with all that you already know and being able to use your wisdom and experience in a new life. What could be better than that?

God, what do I need to do to make this happen? It seems like such a simple question with such a predictable response: spend time with you every day. I've heard that so many times, and I keep on starting up again. The challenge is in sustaining it.

Do I ever live in the moment when things are good in my relationship with you and with others, or am I in a constant state of frustration because it's never good enough? I'm reminded again of the words "I am enough," which caused me indescribable pain when I didn't believe they were really for me. Is that the struggle I have in relationships, that I don't believe that I am enough?

God, am I discounting who you are in our relationship and not giving you credit for accepting me as I am? That song, "Just as I Am," continues to resonate with me. When I sing it, I think I believe it, but now I can see that I don't really internalize it. I'm not enough in my relationship with you. I feel that I'm not fully committed, that I criticize myself because I never spend enough time with you. I get busy with other things and put you on the backburner. Those times when we do connect on a deeper level are usually taken at my discretion, not yours.

In your eyes, I realize now that *I am enough*. Whatever I bring to the relationship is what I'm capable of bringing, for whatever reason, in spite of my circumstances.

You're always waiting, not resentful, dejected, or hurt. You're waiting like the father of the prodigal son, expectant, excited, and delighted when I make my appearance a long way down the road. You're elated as you throw a beautiful coat around me and share your heart. I can imagine you telling me the story of the prodigal. It fills me with an overwhelming sense of your love, acceptance, and deep gratitude for this journey we've taken together.

Chapter Twelve: Breaking down Heart Walls • 163

My child, come on in and let's chat. I've missed you for so long. I want to catch up on what you've been doing. Tell me everything. I'm not here to judge. I just miss you so much. I ached to hold you, and it feels so good to have you in my arms again. I know you'll be leaving on your own business again soon. I wish you would stay at home, that we could spend more time together, but you're a bit of an adventurer, an explorer, and you want to go off in your own direction. I wish you wouldn't because I miss you when you're gone.

I am going to be here when you return. I'll have a new coat waiting for you. I'll throw it around you and we'll sit together, eat together, and laugh together. We may even cry together, for opportunities missed. We'll both wish things could have been different at times.

It doesn't matter. I love you now and will love you forever, with a love that you don't fully understand. It's the love of a father, the love of a mother. Being a parent gives you a tiny glimpse into what that means. I am a God of love, of hope, of forever wishing for you to be the best you can be. I will never leave you or abandon you, no matter where you choose to go in life. I love you, my child.

> *For I know the plans I have for you… plans to give you hope and a future.*
>
> —Jeremiah 29:11

God, I have treasured this verse from Jeremiah. What a gift! It has given me something to hold onto during countless rough times. I've shared it with many others who felt abandoned in life, without a ray of light for the future. I hope it has meant as much to them as it has to me.

My child, when the winds are right, take that hot air balloon ride and fly free. Feel the joy that comes from letting me be part of your life, from daily walking, talking, and yes, even flying together. I will be in the hot air balloon with you when you choose to step into it.

I will fly high with you, proud of what you've done over the past few days, writing from your heart, crying from your heart, laughing from your heart. Most of all, for letting me into your heart to heal the wounds as I open your mind to what you haven't grasped before. I'm always your loving Father and friend, never letting you down, never rejecting you, and always believing in you.

I give you the gift of unencumbered flight. Let your heart wounds go. Leave them behind. I have released the ropes holding you back. Fly free, my child, fly free.

> *I have heard your prayer and seen your tears; I will heal you.*
> —2 Kings 20:5

Afterword

God never wastes a hurt.

—Rick Warren[42]

Rick Warren has often said that we are all broken, but that God never wastes a hurt. I know now that we can learn and grow from our brokenness. We can use it for good in our lives and the lives of others, not letting the hurt be wasted. We can let God turn our mess into an inspiring message that will bring hope and encouragement to others.

Sadly, it has taken over fifty years for me to come to a point in my life where I can say I truly believe that I'm healed from the hurt of my brokenness, especially from when my mother took her life. I didn't even realize I was broken, but the hurt from those fifty-plus years affected my life in many negative ways.

Thankfully, in the midst of my ongoing brokenness, God didn't waste the hurt I was going through. He gave me a passion for hurting people. He gave me insights into the pain of those experiencing

---

42 Rick Warren, *The Purpose-Driven Life: What on Earth Am I Here For?* (Grand Rapids, MI: Zondervan, 2002), 246.

depression. He made it possible for me to minister to other broken people who needed to connect with someone who had walked in their shoes and understood a little about their pain.

After having written this book, I look back and see that the threads of God's goodness and love have always been a part of the tapestry of my life. Those threads are interwoven with the threads of pain caused by my mother's actions. On looking back, I picture a mixture of colors—white threads of deep and pure love, black threads of darkness and despair, yellow threads of joy and laughter, and red threads of hurt, betrayal, and pain.

More and more, as I gaze on that tapestry, I see that some threads have intensified and others have diminished before my eyes. The black and red threads gradually faded during the time I wrote this book. The shades of white, to me a symbol of God's love, and yellow, representing joy, have deepened into rich hues.

My feelings toward my mother have changed to feelings of love. How can I explain what has happened? It has come about only through God's love. As I came to appreciate him walking with me in my journey, I also came to realize that I no longer have feelings of disdain toward my mother. I have only overwhelming love for someone I lost as a little child, someone who has now expanded my heart, which was blocked for so long. This woman deserved compassion in her walk on Earth, but received little understanding and support in the midst of her struggles.

When I became a young adult, my dad gave me my mother's diamond engagement ring. It meant nothing at the time and through the ensuing years. I even took it to a jeweler at one point to see what it was worth. I considered selling it and spending the money on clothes or shoes, which were of more value than a trinket to remember a mother I would have preferred to forget.

I kept the ring, locked up in a safety deposit box with a few other items. I never had a desire to look at it or hold it in my hand. But after I had finished this story, I felt a longing, an urging that I needed to address. I needed to go and bring home that ring—that piece of my mother—to symbolize our union in spirit. I know that I want and need to honor her.

I hope that my mother felt some measure of the love of God as she fought her unending battles and succumbed to the darkness. Before her last goodbye on Earth, I hope she heard God whisper to her as he held her close, "My child, I love you with a never-ending love. I will never leave you or abandon you."

I long to someday hold her in my own arms in the presence of God as I say, "I love you, Mother. I love you. In spite of your own brokenness, you taught me so much that I needed to learn. Forgive me for not understanding you before. God didn't waste your hurt. He didn't waste my hurt. I love you, *Mom*. I love you. I am now proud to call you by that name."

> *If you want your life to be a magnificent story, then begin by realizing that you are the author and every day you have the opportunity to write a new page.*
>
> —Mark Houlahan[43]

---

43 Mark Houlahan, *Goodreads*, "Mark Houlahan Quotes," January 13, 2014 (https://www.goodreads.com/author/quotes/1887121.Mark_Houlahan).

Today I close the door to the past, open the door to the future, take a deep breath, step on through, and start a new chapter in my life.

—Unknown

About the Author

Bonnie's personal and spiritual journey has given words to her life purpose: "I am a joyful, confident, and trusting woman of God, touching people's lives with love and shining a light to bring hope in the darkness."

Bonnie is a former elementary school teacher and adult educator. She has also worked in a senior management position in a provincial education ministry in Canada for twenty-five years.

Her personal writing has been coupled with professional writing and editing for politicians and government bureaucrats. This still left Bonnie with an often-spoken desire to someday write a book. The yearning has now been fulfilled.

Mental health issues and suicide in her immediate family, along with her experience with bipolar disorder, expanded Bonnie's heart and mind to the suffering of others. She has researched the topic of mental health extensively. Bonnie is intuitively tuned to hurting teens and adults who cry out on social media to a world largely insensitive to the pain disguised in their words. She has connected with hundreds of depressed or suicidal individuals. Several have told her that she literally saved their lives.

Bonnie enjoys being outdoors, as well as the adrenaline rush of exploring adventurous new activities. Indoors, she is most often found in front of her computer or a book. Besides visiting her daughter in California, she enjoys travelling to attend a variety of professional and personal growth conferences. She takes more than her share of sunset pictures when she is near an ocean.

Bonnie can be found on various social media platforms where she connects with individuals with similar passions—writing and publishing, mental health, grief recovery, inspired living, and most importantly, a God who loves his children through it all.

Bonnie desires that her writing will touch you with the unconditional love of God and bring you into a deeper relationship with him.

To learn more about Bonnie, visit her website:
www.bonniejbrooks.com

Resource Links

As several chapters of this book focus on mental health issues, the following links are provided to support those dealing with these kinds of challenges, either themselves or with family members or friends.

Canada

Canadian Alliance on Mental Illness and Mental Health (CAMIMH): www.camimh.ca

Canadian Association for Suicide Prevention (CASP): www.suicideprevention.ca

Canadian Mental Health Association (CMHA): www.cmha.ca/bins/index.asp

Centre for Suicide Prevention: www.suicideinfo.ca

Depression Hurts: www.depressionhurts.ca

Mental Health Commission of Canada (MHCC):
www.mentalhealthcommission.ca

Mood Disorders Society of Canada (MDSC):
www.mooddisorderscanada.ca

UNITED STATES

American Mental Health Foundation (AMHF):
www.americanmentalhealthfoundation.org

American Psychiatric Association (APA):
www.psych.org

Depression and Bipolar Support Alliance (DBSA):
www.dbsalliance.org

Mental Health America (MHA): www.nmha.org

Metanoia: Turn toward the Light: www.metanoia.org

National Alliance on Mental Illness (NAMI):
www.nami.org

National Institute of Mental Health (NIMH):
www.nimh.nih.gov

National Suicide Prevention Lifeline:
www.suicidepreventionlifeline.org

Acknowledgements

I offer simple but heartfelt appreciation to the following for their part in bringing this book to life:

Tom Bird, my writing coach and best-selling author, who led me through a five-day writing retreat, which was a life-changing experience. It wasn't what I expected, but more than I imagined. Tom didn't give up on me, even when I complained more than once that my work was inadequate. His gentle and encouraging approach, amazing awareness of the needs of each student, and exceptional insights into the writer's craft made me feel more confident as I crossed over into the world of becoming an author. He was truly a compassionate midwife in helping me to birth this book.

Thelma Box, founder of Choices Seminars, who helped me to understand that we are all responsible for the choices we make. Choices brought me to a turning point as I learned that every one of us needs medicine for healing, but we must be open enough to communicate that need if we want others to help us. I'm also grateful that Thelma took the time to review my manuscript and write the foreword.

Faye McLeod, my oldest sister, who embarked on a writing journey with me to fulfill a common lifelong dream of becoming authors. Her dedication to writing, as well as her encouragement and feedback, motivated me to keep working toward my goal. In spite of difficult circumstances in her own life, Faye learned to discover and be grateful for the goodness in everything, which has inspired me to do the same.

Linda Stepaniuk, my youngest sister, who reminded me at a significant milestone why I should continue my writing journey. When I questioned on my blog about carrying on with the manuscript, she commented, "To follow your dream, you must have faith in the gift God gave you when he answered your prayer and courage to follow your dream to 'write a book from the heart that would offer hope and inspiration to those who chose to read it.'"

Jack Canfield, co-author of the *Chicken Soup for the Soul* series and multiple New York Times best-selling author, who re-ignited my desire to complete this book. Jack said that if a book were to impact only one person's life, it would be worth publishing it. That simple but powerful statement was a turning point for me, leading me to resurrect the manuscript that had lain untouched in my computer for almost a year.

Sheri Kaye Hoff, best-selling author, who also lost a younger brother to suicide and, as a result, understands and appreciates the long-lasting effects of such a tragedy. Sheri carefully read my manuscript and provided insightful, detailed written and verbal feedback to assist me in strengthening the message I was trying to convey.

Lori Zeltwanger, a myofascial release physiotherapist, who supported me in the writing process as she worked with me on various major physical issues every day of the writing retreat. Lori both listened and offered her own exceptional perceptions as we explored my breakthroughs about healing.

Melissa Prokop, my physiotherapist for almost eighteen months after my fall, whose positive attitude helped me break through the darkness to see the sun shine again. Melissa worked aggressively on my physical injuries and taught me pain management techniques to reduce the unrelenting symptoms of complex regional pain syndrome. She believed in me, challenged me, and pushed me hard when needed. She also listened to my dreams and encouraged my passion for writing. Without her, I wouldn't have been physically able to write this book.

And finally, other members of the Normed Therapy team in Sherwood Park, Alberta: Charlotte Dowhaniuk, Allison Gaudet, Dianna Linton, and Erica Stilman. Without their incredible professional support during my extensive physiotherapy, acupuncture, massage therapy, and kinesiology treatments, the words of this book would still remain inside me.

www.ingramcontent.com/pod-product-compliance
Lightning Source LLC
Chambersburg PA
CBHW031257110426
42743CB00040B/714